PATRICE D. HORN / JACK C. HORN

SEX IN THE OFFICE

ADDISON-WESLEY PUBLISHING COMPANY

Reading, Massachusetts • Menlo Park, California

London • Amsterdam • Don Mills, Ontario • Sydney

Library of Congress Cataloging in Publication Data

Horn, Patrice D.
  Sex in the office.

  Includes index.
  1. Executives—Sexual behavior.   2. Sex in business.
I. Horn, Jack C.   II. Title.
HF5500.2.H65   306.7   82-6684
ISBN 0-201-10264-1   AACR2

ISBN 0-201-10264-1

ABCDEFGHIJ-DO-85432

COVER DESIGN BY MARSHALL HENRICHS

For Tony, Lisa, and Andrew

ACKNOWLEDGMENTS

Many people, friends and strangers alike, gave us invaluable help in researching and writing the book. We thank them all. Specifically, T George Harris, who first suggested the project, then provided periodic pep talks to keep us going. To Ryan Vollmer, whose interviews were particularly useful in the sections on sexual harassment, and Lisa Horn, who typed several versions of each chapter, our special thanks and love.

Ann Curran, David Maxey, Berkeley Rice, Heidi Sigel, and Maggie Wolf provided specific information when it was needed and friendly ears when they were essential.

There are others, most of whom we have never met personally, whose writings and ideas provided the background and inspiration for our thinking. They include Rosabeth Moss Kanter, Michael Korda, Michael Maccoby, Margaret Mead, and Robert E. Quinn.

Writing on a subject as controversial as sex in the office, it was sometimes necessary to protect the privacy of the men and women who discussed their personal experiences with us. In these cases, we have changed the names of individuals and companies but kept the other essentials—job classifications, situations, company sizes and types—intact. We thank everyone who helped us anonymously, as well as the management and personnel people who were willing to speak for the record.

Finally, we give special thanks to the people at Addison-Wesley and particularly to Doe Coover, whose patience, good humor, and pertinent editing made her a joy to work with.

CONTENTS

ONE

SEX IN THE OFFICE

To me, the amount of sexual attraction is tremendous. Women dress better. They have more money, they are more visible. Hormones will be hormones.

EXECUTIVE OF THE MULTIFOODS CORP.
Wall St. Journal, April 1981

It's very difficult—I spend ten hours a day with the guys I work with. That's three times what I spend with my husband. The whole system is set up to foster involvements.

YOUNG WOMAN RESEARCHER
Glamour magazine, March 1981

1

EX IN THE OFFICE isn't a new phenomenon. It has been going on since men and women started working together. But while the act is the same, the attitudes and atmosphere surrounding it have changed tremendously in the last decade or so. The revolutions of the 1970s and 1980s—the women's movement, sexual liberation, the restructured American family—have changed the complexion of the relationship between men and women in the office.

In offices today you find young, attractive, well-educated women who have arrived on the work scene with an entirely different set of expectations and values from those held by previous generations. They expect to have successful careers, to be independent, to have exciting sex lives, and *not* to be judged by moral or economic standards from the dark ages. At the same time many men are experiencing sharp changes in their dealings with other men as well as with women, involving greater friendship and less competition. All in all, we are in the midst of a major transition—a movement toward equality between the sexes both on the job and in the bed.

For many men and women, the corporation is well on its way to replacing the family as a source of affection, community, and support. We separate from our biological families in our twenties and find replacement families at our jobs. We socialize with co-workers, confide in them, trust them with our problems, and share our joys with them. So it is natural that men and women both turn to the office to find prospective mates—short-term or long-term.

Just as individual men and women are trying to cope with and understand these changes, so the corporate structure must absorb and react to them. Hiring more women and promoting them more equitably is only a start. Relationships between the sexes on the job must be acknowledged and dealt with in light of today's atmosphere of freedom and equality. Companies simply cannot expect people to live by one standard outside the office and another on the job.

These new attitudes have created situations and occasional problems that management must face and find sensible ways of handling. If a manager sees promise in an attractive woman and helps her up the ladder of corporate success, must it always result in rumors that she slept her way to the top? Must all friendships between men and women be suspect? Must any romantic interest in co-workers be proscribed?

Ideally, companies will learn to create an atmosphere in which men and women are free to conduct their private lives as they choose, without fear of rejection or reprisal by the company or fellow employees. But the corporate signals are mixed. The 1980s may turn the boardroom into a bedroom, or we may see a return to the old corporate rules that at one time outlawed even dating between co-workers. For some observers, like author-publisher Michael Korda, whose self-help books on how to succeed and how to gain power were best-sellers in the 1970s, the office in the 1980s will be an exciting and invigorating place. In a *Playboy* Magazine article on "Sexual Office Politics," he predicted that two things will happen as more women join the executive ranks: the politics will get tougher and the sex will get terrific. During the

Kissinger years in Washington, we heard that power is the ultimate aphrodisiac—in other words, power, not good looks, was what women found sexy about men. Today, Korda points out, power is a direct aphrodisiac for women too; the more power women gain, the sexier they become. "They have discovered that it [power] is not only the next best thing to sex, but is closely linked to sex. Power, in short, feels good. And while it may be nice to be taken out to dinner, or even to bed, by a powerful man, it's even better to beat him at his own game, which is the real high of the 1980s, or better still, to go to bed with him *and* beat him at his own game."

Korda suggests that women who have gained power can be tougher in-fighters than the men they deal with. A willingness to use their sexuality to get what they want can be part of their strength. These women, Korda says, know their business, refuse to put up with sexual put-downs—they are in the enviable position of not having to do so—and don't hesitate to chop a man off at the knees if the situation warrants. They enjoy their power, and their equality on the business front makes for equality on the sexual front—one of the more exciting prospects of the 1980s.

A woman executive told Korda how she sees corporate business and sex in the coming years: "The competition is going to get a lot hotter, and . . . when women are competing equally with men, you are probably going to have better sex. Women have always used sex as a substitute for power, a way of fighting back; and men have thought of sex as a way of keeping women in their place. Sex between equals. Now that's a revolutionary idea."

This breezy projection opts for the fun of the hunt, but not everyone agrees that bed and business can be mixed so easily or so equally. The late anthropologist

Margaret Mead felt that the changing role of women has given the corporation a new responsibility to control sexual goings-on within its walls. Writing in *Redbook* Magazine in 1979, Mead pointed out that attitudes toward sexual freedom and women's rights are changing. ''Taboos break down in periods of transition. We are in such a period now. And like the family, the modern business and modern profession must develop incest taboos. If women are to work on an equal basis with men, with men supervising women in some cases and women supervising men in others, we have to develop decent sex mores in the whole working world. . . .

''What we need, in fact are new taboos that will operate within the work setting as once they operated within the household. Neither men nor women should expect that sex can be used either to victimize women who need to keep their jobs, or to keep women from advancement, or to help men advance their own careers. A taboo enjoins. We need one that says clearly and unequivocally, 'You don't make passes at or sleep with the people you work with.' ''

Dr. Mead pointed to the universities as an example of what can and should be done along these lines. ''Today, wherever there is coeducation with a fairly even ratio between the sexes and several years' experience of living in coeducational dormitories, a quiet taboo is developing without the support of formal rules and regulations, fines or public exposure, praise or censure—a taboo against serious dating within the dormitory. Young women and young men who will later have to work side by side, in superordinate and subordinate relations as well as equals and members of a team, are finding their way toward a kind of harmony in which exploitive sex is set aside in favor of mutual concern, shared interests and, it seems to me, a new sense of friendship.''

As Dr. Mead stated, this is just a beginning. ''But the commitment and acceptance that are implied by taboos are critical in the formation and protection of the most meaningful human relations.''

Most management and career counselors for women would agree with Dr. Mead, and many go further, advising women to take Caesar's wife as their role model—not only remaining pure but, just as important, being careful to maintain the appearance of purity.

So much for theory and advice. Let us take a look at what has actually happened during the last decade to women and to sexual mores—the two forces of change in the corporate world.

The 1970s reaped the harvest sown in the 1960s by the sexual revolution and the women's movement. Together, these profound sociological changes are responsible for the new freedom, and the abuse of this freedom, that exist in the work world today. Although the advances women have made are small in some respects, many women have moved into new positions of responsibility—a vantage point that has made most of them aware of how far they have to go. These women, who make up a growing part of the work force, have career desires and aspirations equal to those of the men they work with, even if their successes are not as yet equal.

Women are changing roles as well as goals in their lives. These changes are particularly strong among the baby-boom women born from the mid–1940s through the mid–1950s. Many of these thirty-seven million women, now in their prime career years, are marrying later than their foremothers did and have delayed having children until their education was finished and their careers established. Although in the United States the majority of babies are born to women under thirty, in this group there has been a 15 percent increase in the birth rate for women over thirty. Many others of these women are simply not getting married, opting either to stay single or to cohabitate without ceremony. Among those already married, the divorce rate has grown astronomically and the number of households headed by women has increased dramatically. All these changes point to one thing: women are no longer dependent on men for their upkeep or their social position.

The force of these changes can be seen clearly in the dramatic change in the sexual ratio in the workplace. Women are entering and staying in the job market in progressively larger numbers and for increasingly longer periods of time. A recent Labor Department study called this influx of women "the most significant phenomenon of the last 30 years." In 1950, women accounted for less than 30 percent of the American work force. Today, the figure is approaching 50 percent. Among women 25 to 34, 65 percent are working. Although the majority (55 percent) of employed women still work in traditionally female clerical and service jobs, a substantial number have made inroads into technical, professional, and managerial positions. Bureau of Labor Statistics show that since 1970, the proportion of women has increased from 26 percent to 33 percent in accounting; from 5 percent to 12 percent in law; from 9 percent to 11 percent in medicine; from 1.6 percent to 2.9 percent in engineering; and from 17 to 25 percent in management.

These are impressive increases, but the future appears even brighter when you look at the educational strides made by women in the last decade. In 1970, women received only 13 percent of the doctoral degrees awarded by American universities. Eight years later, the number was up to 24 percent, and climbing. During this same time, women made even greater advances, proportionally, in traditionally male doctoral fields; for instance, in engineering the increase was from 0.7 to 2.8 percent, and in the physical sciences the increase was from 5.4 to 9.5 percent. Figures for Master of Business Administration degrees—the key to the executive suite—are just as impressive. In 1971, women received 4 percent of the MBAs awarded; in 1979, they accounted for 19 percent. Similarly, the number of Bachelor of Arts and Master of Science degrees obtained by women increased in the 1970s.

These advances in work-force participation and education are indications of how motivated women are to achieve equality on the job, as well as elsewhere. They want more money and more status and are acquiring the skills and resources needed to obtain them.

To put it simply, there is a new woman on the business scene today—one who is not about to take a back seat to anyone. She not only asks for a piece of the pie but demands her legal right to it. This new-found confidence is related to the sexual freedom women gained through the development of the pill and other effective, easily available forms of birth control, as well as the legalization of abortion. With little fear of pregnancy, women have been able to enjoy sex on its own merits, much as men have always done. As a result, in the 1970s sex became an accepted form of recreation for more women than ever before. This shift in attitude and action had a more subtle effect on the corporation than it did on the college campus, but the results were much the same. The big difference was that discretion was still the rule in the office, while a "let it all hang out" philosophy held sway on many campuses. Sex was in, promiscuity was accepted, and morality—or at least the face of morality, as practiced by previous generations—was passé. Women were finally able to say out loud, "I like sex," follow up their words with deeds, and not be thought of as scarlet women.

Sex became a prime topic in the media, and the so-called singles scene—in which the "single" was often married but out on the town alone—was likened to a giant market, with everyone hawking his or her wares. The one-night stand became a standard part of the evening's entertainment, no more unusual than a predinner cocktail or a postdinner movie. With all this sexual freedom after hours, it was bound to crop up in the office. And it did, with a vengeance.

Sex, potential and actual, is an important element in today's office. It affects how men treat women, how women respond, and how women initiate affairs on their own. Sexual habits, inclinations, and preferences are often openly discussed, accepted, and acted upon by both sexes. In this permissive climate, sexual liaisons of all kinds flourish, with either sex likely to lead the way. Equality in and out of bed is the goal if not the fully realized reality.

Although many people see this new sexual freedom in the office as a pure joy, others warn of its pitfalls, particularly for career-minded women. The decision to stand on her own two feet and compete in what is still a largely male-dominated world demands more than time, dedication, and energy from an ambitious woman; it also can make saying "no" to office romance a virtue. The old male adage of "Don't fish off the company pier" is considered by many to be doubly good advice for women on the way up, and those who hope to be. Climbing the company ladder rung by rung is a lot surer for a woman than trying it bed by bed—though a successful rung-climber is likely to be suspected of using sex for advancement whatever route she takes.

10

Given that most men would rather not be labeled male chauvinist pigs (or worse) you might expect romance to have flown out the company window. But just the reverse seems to be happening. Hormones are still hormones, and the attractions of sex are as strong as ever. In fact, many of the changes that have taken place in the office have made life there more sexually titillating than ever, as well as considerably more complicated. For men, the old rules have changed. What some men consider common courtesy, or an attempt at gallantry—such as offering to buy a woman dinner and escort her home after a late work night —is now often viewed by women in the cold, clear light of liberation and found to be sexist and patronizing. The romantic gesture, particularly popular with older men, can boomerang with unexpected force and anger, making them feel that they have somehow slipped out of this century into some alien time, where men are no longer men and women are God knows what.

The office scene can be just as confusing for a young man who, expecting that equality, with its combination of camaraderie and competition, is a turn-on for both sexes, gets slapped down when he makes an overture. The woman who delights in sexual banter in a bar or at a party may well throw a karate chop, verbal or otherwise, at the man who acts the same way in the office.

This uncertainty can be frustrating for even the best-intentioned man; for the less well-intentioned, it is infuriating. On the one hand, there are exciting, liberated, sexually emancipated women, oozing with sex appeal and ready for action. On the other hand, there are exciting, liberated women, equally appealing, who will not tolerate sexual or sexist remarks, much less any physical follow-up. They are in the office to work, to progress, and to be accepted as a person, not a sex object. How do you tell one type from the other without a scorecard, and without an occasional error?

One young executive gave us his view of the dilemma: "It's sometimes like being a diabetic in a candy store. Look but don't touch. And in some cases, don't even look, or if you do, for God's sake don't get caught. And never, never voice your attraction.

"I really do respect what women want to accomplish, but I can't deny an occasional urge. Maybe we could develop some new office version of the old Hawaiian custom of girls wearing flowers behind one ear if they are available, and the other if they're not. We could substitute a pencil for the flower, with the woman wearing it behind the appropriate ear if she wants to be complimented or dated. It would sure simplify matters. I often feel that I'm damned if I do and damned if I don't when it comes to recognizing a woman for something more than her superlative management qualities." Office relationships can be confusing for a woman too, particularly when the friendly overtures come from her boss or some other man higher up in the corporation structure who could be the mentor she needs. Many writers on business success believe that such a mentor or godfather—someone willing to guide the young employee through the company maze with advice and put in a good word for him or her with the right people—is essential to success in any large business. A young woman who comes down hard on what she views as a sexual or sexist suggestion may find she has aced herself out of just such help. The proverbial form of a woman scorned is easily matched by the anger of a boss rebuffed. Unfortunately it's often difficult to interpret the fine distinctions between harmless and helpful attention and sexual harassment.

Such harassment has recently been acknowledged as

a major problem by the media, the government, and the corporations themselves. It is costly in a number of ways. The most important costs are borne by its victims—psychological trauma, usually, and in extreme cases, physical damage as well. But there are also financial costs. A federal study of sexism in government offices estimates that sexual harassment cost the taxpayer $189 million during the two-year period from May 1978 to May 1980 in terms of job turnover, lost productivity, and health care expense. If such persecution is equally prevalent in private business—certainly a reasonable assumption—the nationwide costs run to tens of billions of dollars yearly.

While women are the usual victims, 15 percent of the men questioned in the government survey reported that they, too, had been sexually harassed at one time or another. It is also clear that the victimizing is often inflicted by supervisors, making it a financial as well as a psychological threat.

One of the first studies of the subject was done by *Redbook* Magazine in 1976, with results that at the time seemed astounding. Nearly nine out of every ten women questioned said they had experienced some form of sexual harassment on the job. While the pressure was sometimes subtle rather than overt, the consequences for resisting it were often serious. Forty-five percent of the women reported that they or a woman they knew had either been fired or quit due to harassment.

Since this pioneering study, the matter has been examined by social scientists and by reporters in all the media, with results that demonstrate how pervasive the phenomenon is. During the 1981 Senate hearings that reviewed new Equal Employment Opportunities Commission guidelines for dealing with the problem, the Center for Women's Policy Studies, a Washington-based research group, estimated that 18 million women were harassed sexually at work during 1979 and 1980.

At the same hearings, antifeminist crusader Phyllis Schlafly labeled these 18 million as provocateurs rather than victims. "Sexual harassment on the job is not a problem for virtuous women," Mrs. Schlafly testified, "except in the rarest of cases. Men hardly ever ask sexual favors of women from whom the certain answer is no. Virtuous women are seldom accosted." She also reminded the Committee to keep in mind that "some women have abandoned the commandments against adultery and fornication." With these temptresses facing him day after day, what could a poor, weak man do but yield to temptation?

Unfortunately, you can't just laugh away the Schlaflys of this world, especially if you work with or for them. Current studies of how corporations handle complaints by women show that many executives dismiss harassment as either a minor annoyance or a figment of the victim's imagination. *Redbook* again led the way by joining the *Harvard Business Review* in a survey, published in May 1981, of how men and women managers view harassment. They found, unsurprisingly, that the women were both more conscious of and more appalled by the problem. Asked to evaluate the statement, "The amount of sexual harassment at work is greatly exaggerated," nearly two-thirds of the male managers agreed, compared to fewer than half the women.

Despite this difference, answers to other questions made it clear that managers of both sexes considered sexual harassment a serious problem, saw that it is often tied to the exercise of power, agreed that top management is usually isolated from the problem, and admitted that, with a few exceptions, their companies do not have a well-formed policy to deal with the issue.

How much right a company has to interfere in its people's private lives is debatable. The personnel manager of an electronics firm believed strongly in a hands-off approach: "If two people in my company are friends and end up in bed together that's their business. It's not management's job to dictate morality." However, he also made it clear that sexual innuendo, insulting remarks, or sexual coercion of any kind was a different matter and that employees should be informed that the company is prepared to step in and stop it.

In the *Redbook–Harvard Business Review* study, the managers' responses to a series of statements about company policy revealed a wide discrepancy between what the managers favored and what their companies had actually done. For example, nearly three-quarters of the managers believed that a company should issue a formal statement to all employees decrying sexual harassment, yet only about one-quarter said that their companies had made such a statement. On the other hand, most of the managers objected to any official policy regarding office flirtations or romances. Seventy-five percent felt that this was personal business and that the company should ignore it.

The matter of office flirtation is a no-person's land between sexual harassment and true love—an area that can be filled with equal measures of pleasure and danger for anyone who plays the game. It is also an area that is especially vulnerable to office gossip and resentment as well as a source of vicarious pleasure for the spectators. Having an affair with a co-worker is like undressing in Macy's window: no matter how discreetly it is done, a lot of people know about it.

Sex in the office is really a range of subjects, differing in the involvement of the individuals. For the sake of simplicity, we have divided these into six somewhat arbitrary categories: The lightweight of the group is flirting. It includes sexual banter and body language that can be used on one specific target of the opposite sex or a whole officeful.

The next category is the one-night stand—the brief encounter that usually doesn't reflect any particular planning or caring on either side—just a seized opportunity.

Casual dating between co-workers is another step up the involvement scale. It may include sexual intercourse or not, depending on the individuals.

Next comes the affair. We define this as a long-term, serious sexual relationship between people who may be both single, both married, or one of each. It may be uncomplicated (most likely in the first case) or troublesome (more than likely in the last two cases).

Sexual harassment is a special situation but is serious and common enough to justify being included. Any of the four previous categories can reflect or exemplify sexual harassment when someone in power uses it to gain sexual favors or to put down a person of the opposite sex (or in the case of homosexual harassment, someone of the same sex).

The final category is commitment, which occurs when a liaison leads to marriage or cohabitation of some kind. This relationship is based on mutual love and trust.

The frequency of office ardor, at all these levels, shouldn't surprise us. While offices aren't set up or decorated as passion pits, there are numerous psychological and physical incentives to the development of romance, as well as profits, in any organization. Proximity, for example, is considerably more powerful than most of us realize. The old adage about familiarity breeding contempt does not apply to sexual attraction. The most romantic setting may be a deserted beach in Tahiti, where some enchanted evening you will meet a sexy stranger, but few of us have this opportunity. We usually fall in love with, and marry, the people around us, people who have similar backgrounds, people we see often in ordinary places, such as the office in which we work. This sounds dull, but it isn't if you look at what is going on under the surface.

Practically every emotion you can name—from despair to exultation—is expressed routinely in offices and corridors. Our jobs alternately challenge and frustrate most of us, creating an emotional seesaw that makes an ideal spawning ground for sexual attraction. If you are working on a risky venture with an attractive partner, a project that could make or break you in the company, your adrenalin level is high. You feel good, nervous, excited. The sense of high risk—of doing a high-wire act together—can be easily translated into sexual attraction for your partner.

If you succeed, you feel terrific. A rosy glow fills the world, and you are ready to celebrate. If you fail, you are wretched and crave consolation. Either way, the one person who knows and understands all that has happened and all that was at stake is close by, just as involved and feeling just as you do at that moment. Falling into one another's arms seems right and natural.

The same forces are at work, at a lower pitch, when men and women share everyday challenges and annoyances on the job: hating the boss; competing to see who can make the most suggestions at a meeting; sharing the need-to-relax feeling after working late; the camaraderie of a business trip in an exciting city—or a dull one, in which case the need for some personally generated excitement is even stronger. All these work involvements can lead to sexual involvement. The fact is, the office is a sexy place. Ask anyone who has worked both in largely single-sex offices and in ones in which men and women work side by side. They will tell you that the former setting is duller, more competitive in a negative way, and less stimulating all around.

"Men make me feel good. I'm funnier, sharper, and feel more competent with them around," reported a woman editor who had experienced both worlds of work. She wasn't putting women down, she said, but just admitting honestly that she preferred working with both sexes.

A California man who spent many years in a nearly all-male engineering department in the aerospace industry felt the same way. "I missed the banter, the humor and, quite honestly, the girls in their summer dresses. I think we tend to show off a little more, to be at the top of our form when there are women around. It just makes work more fun, less rigid and demanding."

What these people are talking about—the enjoyment and excitement of the opposite sex—is the best of all working worlds, but it is best only when it is egalitarian rather than exploitative. This is one reason the idea of company rules against dating fellow employees seems so archaic. Women and men don't need *protection* from each other; they need *respect* for each other. This does not necessarily mean seeing everyone as nonsexual; it means seeing them as equals. And if this leads to sex, romance, or both, so be it. Whether the result is an affair, a fling, or merely a flirtation, it can be good for what ails us. The sexual atmosphere in the office can be exciting, and many enjoy their part in creating it. For them, sex is fun, flings are where you find them—and even love can flourish among the files.

The people working in offices today—especially the younger ones—are ready for this kind of equal relationship, organizational and sexual. It is up to today's companies, and the managers who interpret company policies, to replace the locker-room atmosphere that pervades most of America's corporate headquarters with a spirit of freedom and equality that matches the times. In the long run, this spirit will benefit both the businesses and the people who work for them.

Whether the office will become the new battleground of the sexes or the spawning ground for better-than-ever sexual relationships is what this book is about. In the following chapters, we will look in depth at the question of office sex in the 1980s, not with the idea of suggesting how to prevent, cure, or cultivate it but simply to examine all sides of the phenomenon—the good and the bad, the humorous and the serious.

TWO

LOOKING FOR LOVE & EXCITEMENT

2

WHATEVER FORM IT TAKES, a sexual liaison in the office has a motive behind it. Individuals bring their emotional needs and quirks to work with them; they don't leave them home or park them outside the door from nine to five. For convenience, we have divided the motives underlying most romantic relationships into three areas: the desire for love, the desire for excitement, and the desire for power.

Most of us realize that it takes more than a successful career to make life fulfilling. We all also want a little excitement and a lot of love, or vice versa. The simplest way to satisfy these needs is to combine work, love, and/or excitement on the job. Others use sex as a way to gain power and help them get what they want in their careers. People looking for love and excitement through office liaisons usually don't create as many problems in the office as the power seekers. Their liaisons simply don't arouse the same concern and opposition, since fellow workers don't feel as threatened as they do by women and men who use sex and romance as a career ploy (see Chapter 6 on co-workers' reactions to office affairs).

There is a difference between relationships based on the desire for love and those based on the desire for excitement, although both elements can be part of the same relationship, particularly at its beginning. Love involves a variety of complex feelings built on a rather simple biological base, what some have called ''the tyranny of the DNA''—the neurological pull men and women feel toward each other. Psychiatrist Ted Nadelson calls this attraction ''a hard-wired phenomenon. We've forgotten that it's been in our brains for two and a half million years. It is necessary for species generation and we are always aware of it, if only subconsciously.'' Nadelson points out that from a simple biological standpoint ''individuals really don't matter in the long flow of evolution. All that counts is that we reproduce ourselves. To paraphrase Samuel Butler's aphorism—'a chicken is an egg's way of making more eggs'—a human being is DNA's way of making more DNA.'' Dr. Nadelson isn't saying that our desire for sex and love are purely biological drives, but he is reminding us that we are biological creatures with deep and strong basic needs.

Relationships between men and women today, however, are as much social and psychological as they are physiological. We have evolved a complex set of needs and desires that can't be explained so simply. From the time we are born, we crave love and closeness from others. From psychologist Harry Harlow's pioneering work with monkeys to the research reported by anthropologist Ashley Montagu in his recent book *Touching,* studies have shown that physical contact or the lack of it has a strong effect on how well we grow, physically and emotionally. Praise and encouragement—what might be called ''psychic touching''—are equally necessary to complete this development.

Given the strong human need for contact and affection, it is not surprising that sex rears its lovely head so regularly in the office. Most of us spend about as much waking time at work, among our peers and bosses, as we do everywhere else put together. For anyone seeking love, the halls, offices, and cafeterias of our office buildings are logical places to look. The strong emotions that develop on and under the surface during the work day can easily be translated into attraction and, with enough time and the proper chemistry, into love. There is little difference between meeting your loved-one-to-be at the file cabinet or on an ocean cruise. Office romance is just a bit more complicated, surrounded as it is by certain taboos and the sometimes smothering interest of fellow workers.

Working closely with someone you like can be tremendously fulfilling. The trust that develops when people work together, the satisfaction of watching others develop their talents or of feeling your own abilities grow, the shared satisfaction that comes from a job well done— these can be the basis for a mutual respect that gradually turns to love. In many ways, offices are ideal places for love to begin; there are few situations in which you learn as much about individuals as you do by working with them. This is especially true today, since (as we explain more fully in Chapter 7), the workplace has for many of us replaced the family as our chief source of support and affection.

The need for love and affection can be expressed sexually in varying degrees: from mild flirtations to cohabitation and marriage. You often see flirting by young people who have been popular in high school or college and are accustomed to being sought after, the center of attention. Their first taste of the impersonal business world can be disappointing. Flirting is one avenue open to regain the attention and affection they miss. Young women who have been babied and petted by their families are likely to use flirting in the same way, replacing their loving families with a loving man or two. Young men who miss being the center of attention use flirting the same way.

One big difference between office flirts who simply

want people to like them and flirts who are after power is that the staff and the boss usually react much more positively to the first type. Their ingenuousness wins friendship rather than opposition. Nobody gets hurt; in fact, some male bosses feel innocent flirting creates a friendly, playful mood that helps ease the normal day-to-day office tensions.

The same favorable results are produced by dating, the next step up the office intimacy ladder, when the dates are based on mutual attraction rather than some darker motive. As long as the daters keep things light and friendly, the effect they have on others in the office is likely to be beneficial. Problems can arise at some companies if the attraction continues to grow and the lovers decide to get married. Recent surveys indicate that about 15 percent of U.S. businesses still have a policy of not employing both members of a married couple, although some have relaxed their no-marriage rules by providing for a less severe penalty than dismissal. Couples can continue to work for the company after they marry, just so they are not in the same department or—to avoid any suspicion of favoritism—in positions where one is in a supervisory position over the other. We haven't heard of any corporations that have similar formal policies against cohabitation without marriage, but this seems to be a matter of omission—not keeping company policy manuals up with the times—rather than any conscious decision in favor of sin over ceremony.

Relaxation of company rules against marrying or even dating people in the same office is a move in the right direction, but the times demand much more. Even informal discouragement is a clear example of management trying to apply old rules to new situations. There are plenty of man/woman cases in which company action is justified or even necessary—such as when someone takes advantage of a sexual relationship to gain a promotion or win some other job benefit (we'll talk about this in the next chapter). Or the more serious matter of sexual harassment (discussed in Chapter 4), in which someone—usually a male—uses his position to obtain sex or whatever sexual satisfaction he can from suggestive or obscene remarks. Company action to stop such actions is both needed and desirable, but it should be restricted to such cases. Sexual relationships between two consenting adults are none of the company's business.

Rules that discourage marriage between employees present an obvious dilemma to men and women who start dating casually and then find themselves falling in love. Faced with the prospect of losing a job, or at least narrowing future job prospects, men and women are leery about becoming involved with a fellow worker in the first place; or, if they do get involved, they are secretive about it—a hard thing to achieve when so many people seem to have a special skill at sniffing out budding love affairs. Keeping things quiet is made even more difficult by our natural desire to be with the people we love and share our happiness with office friends.

One couple who successfully managed to run the entire romantic course, from flirting through living together, did so without arousing suspicion in a company where it could have hurt their job prospects. They eventually married after both moved on to better positions with other companies. Louise, who now is a promotional director for a fashion agency, met Harry when they were both employed by a well-known business machine manufacturer. Louise was a manager in one of the company's sales departments at corporate headquarters in Connecticut. As part of her job, she occasionally visited the New

York office, where Harry had recently been hired as a salesman.

Their early meetings were anything but romantic, at least in Louise's eyes. She felt that Harry was too pushy and aggressive in trying to date her; and in any case, she had a firm rule against going out with people she worked with. "From what I had seen around the office," she told us, "it just seemed to me that work and personal life don't mix if you want to get ahead." Not much happened until Harry was transferred to the home office for a month of special training. At a party for the salesmen, Louise and Harry found a great common interest—music. Louise had organized a jazz band to play at the party, and Harry, hearing about this, brought his guitar along and joined in. According to him, "Louise couldn't resist my beautiful voice." They left the party together, drove down to his New York apartment and, according to Louise, "haven't separated since."

For a year, before they changed jobs, Louise lived with Harry in New York and commuted to her job in Connecticut. They kept their relationship secret because it seemed that at least one of them would have been fired if it became known. Harry was the more likely candidate, since he hadn't been with the company long, and Louise was higher up in the organization. But her job could have been in jeopardy too, for in her position she had access to special information that would have given Harry an advantage over the other salesmen if she had shared it with him. Obviously this arrangement could not go on forever, particularly since Louise and Harry were seriously in love and wanted to marry. Their jobs were important to them, but not as important as their relationship. After about a year, they both found new jobs and were married.

Most companies, fortunately for office romance, don't

object to employees marrying, and couples who work for these companies often find that the shared experience adds something to their relationship. Linda Wolfe reported in *New York* Magazine, for example, that men and women who work in the same field have a better understanding of both the pressures and the excitement of their spouse's job. A survey by Time, Inc., of its married employees found that most of them considered working for the same company a positive feature. Ralph Graves, editorial director of the corporation, had this to say about his wife of 23 years, Elinor, an executive editor of *LIFE*: "If she came home and talked about IBM, I'd be less interested than I am now. Elinor agreed, "God forbid that I married a physicist." But she pointed out that there were problems, too. "The advantages of working in the same company as your husband are far more personal than professional. It gives you a great base of common interests and it's lovely to share that.

"But for a woman, there is a real disadvantage professionally. There is always the feeling that people are thinking, 'Did she get where she is because her husband is highly placed in that company?'"

When we (the authors of this book) worked for seven years on a newsletter and a magazine together, we discovered a somewhat different advantage: the lack of shop-talk around the home. We didn't need to discuss at dinner what had happened at the office that day; we already knew. One evening, a year or so after we started working together, we realized how different this was from what went on when we worked for different firms. Something particularly interesting had happened at the office, and we were eagerly discussing it during dinner. Our young daughter, Lisa, listened patiently for a while and then, when there was a moment's silence, broke in exasperatedly, ''You two are doing it again!'' When we asked what she meant, Lisa replied, ''Talking to each other about work, and ignoring us. You haven't done that in a long time.'' That's when we realized that, for us and our children, one advantage of working together was the chance to leave the job at the office most of the time, giving us more time to devote to the rest of the family.

This is the good side of working together. It can have its problems too, personally and for the company at which a couple works. For the couple, being together virtually twenty-four hours a day can be wearing on even the warmest relationship. And if the husband and wife have an argument, at home or at work, there is no separation for a cooling-off period.

For the company that employs the couple, there is always the possibility that one spouse will favor the other, causing problems among the people they work with. Even if this never really occurs, the suspicion of favoritism can be nearly as damaging to morale. There is also the danger that if one spouse quits to take a job in another city, or is fired, the company will lose two employees rather than one. Or if the couple separates or divorces, the enforced closeness at work is uncomfortable for everyone and may be disruptive as people choose sides.

For these reasons some companies either formally ban or informally discourage married couples from working together. But many of the same potential problems exist for a man and woman who become involved in a love affair in the same office. Such affairs vary, but there are two basic categories: the simple, untroubled affairs; and the difficult ones, usually complicated by the presence of a spouse or two waiting at home. In the first type, the man and woman involved are usually single, divorced, or widowed individuals who have an egalitarian relationship in which neither takes advantage of the other for personal gain. These affairs seldom cause trouble for fellow workers or the company, whether they fizzle out, as they usually do, or lead to a more lasting relationship. At worst, if the affair breaks up with one person still caring about the other, working in the same office can be painful for the ex-lovers but is probably not troublesome to anyone else. If the affair does prosper, it often adds a rosy glow to the workplace that lifts staff morale a notch or two.

The second kind of affair more often creates havoc for the people involved and for the people they work with. Usually one or both of the lovers is married. Remember that we aren't talking here about men and women who are simply out to have some fun or to gain some advantage from the relationship but about two people who feel love for one another. The heartache of these affairs is frequently increased by the disapproval of management and their fellow workers. There is also a good chance that at least one of the lovers will be forced to settle for less than 100 percent commitment from the other, who still feels loyalty and perhaps love for his or her spouse.

In these situations, work is likely to suffer. As one man who had gone through such an affair recently told us, ''It's not easy, when you still have deep feelings for your wife, and yet you're in love with a woman in the office. It really tore me apart—I guess it did her, too. I know I wasn't doing a very good job, either. I just had too many things on my mind.''

The surveys we have seen that ask about extramarital affairs confirm the obvious: married women who work have more affairs than wives who stay home. This is not too surprising, since women at home have a considerably smaller pool of men to choose from. For example, a *Redbook* Magazine survey on women's sexuality reported that while 29 percent of all the married women questioned admitted having had extramarital sex, the percentage increased dramatically for women who held full-time jobs. Among those in their late thirties, for instance, more than half the working women had affairs compared to only 24 percent of housewives. In a recent survey by *Self* Magazine, 26 percent of its readers who responded said they had had an "office affair."

Marriage is only one complication that besets office affairs. The fishbowl atmosphere can have a dampening effect on the fiercest flames as lovers feel the need to escape the prying eyes of co-workers. Some couples establish firm rules about how they act in the office. One couple, who work in the sales department of an insurance company, say that even when they discuss work, they make sure to keep the door open, sit on opposite sides of the desk, and never, never, touch each other. Otherwise, they know they would be kidded unmercifully. "If I hear one more person calling us 'lovey-dovey,' or say, 'Ah, ah, at it again,' each time I talk to Kevin, I'll scream," Marian says. They both felt that this interference in their personal lives was beginning to affect their relationship and their work. "I think that lately," Kevin says, "we spend more time after work discussing what we can do about this problem than we do thinking about the good times we have had. I guess the rest of the people must lead pretty dull lives if what we do is so damned interesting to them."

This may seem like a minor problem to a man or woman who is juggling the conflicting demands of an office affair and a family at home, but the constant attention of others can be wearing and eventually destructive to the most loving relationship. Office affairs are hard work even when they are based on real love and caring.

Flirting as a natural expression adds spice to office routine in a way that can be positively helpful to office morale and productivity. Gloria Brown Anderson, managing editor of the *Miami News,* is all in favor of a little sexual electricity during the workday. In an interview reported in a *Wall Street Journal* article on sexual tension, she said, "People working together can do very creative work under the influence of mutual infatuation. In some cases the quality of work is improved, because there is something very rich about sharing something with someone who knows you well."

The *Wall Street Journal* article concluded that today's office environment is sexier than ever before. One executive expressed his feelings this way: "Men and women together in close relationships, at work or elsewhere, means a state of risk. There are going to be temptations and sexual attractions, and people are fooling themselves if they don't face that. A man and a woman working together cannot have the same kind of work relationship as two men or two women."

Most offices seem to have at least one man and one woman who are natural flirts. As one man employed in a television station told us, "Cathy never really says yes or no to you. There always seems to be a maybe floating around her." Another man on the same staff offered a longer-range view: "Practically every man on the staff had their own daydreams about her. Some tried, some didn't, and after a while it simmered down. But every time a new guy came along, you could be sure Cathy checked him out, and vice versa."

Admittedly, Cathy was not nearly as popular with women in the office. She was tolerated but not quite trusted, although the women we questioned admitted that Cathy wasn't using her charms for personal advancement. She just liked the excitement she created.

Women in other companies told us about the male flirts they worked with. Most of them agreed that, even when they made no overt moves, these men were fun to have around. According to one happily married secretary, who often daydreamed about her boss but never really wanted or expected anything to happen between them, "I used to get dressed for work with him in mind, and if he noticed and said something, it made my day." Other women told us about crushes they had on men in their office—crushes that made office routine much more bearable.

Crushes and flirting occasionally lead to what in earlier days were called flings. The right circumstances— a joint trip out of town to a convention, an office party, a late night at work—can provide the spark that turns words into action. Usually neither party expects such one-night stands to develop into anything more serious. A fling can turn into an affair, but it usually remains a brief break from routine. After a trip or party during which they became sexually involved, most people—especially women, from what they told us—make sure that ends the matter. As one woman told us, "I couldn't see any future with Jim, except trouble." Most of the men felt the same way: "It was fun, but I've got other things to do."

We uncovered a sharp difference in how the younger women we talked to viewed recreational sex. In general, they were for it—much more than women in their forties or fifties. But office sex—relationships with men they worked with—was a different matter. Their feelings were unlike those of the executive women that Jane Adams reported on in her book *Women at the Top*. She found that women in their twenties and thirties were receptive to the idea of office sex and did not condemn it as many older women executives did.

The young women we spoke to—most of them not as highly placed in their organizations as the women Adams wrote about—were basically against sex in the office. Their objection was not on moral grounds—the women were all in favor of sexual freedom—but they believed that mixing sex with business was not professional; it was not the kind of conduct that would help them get ahead in the business world.

Despite these reservations, many women still see the office as a great place to meet men—certainly better and less dehumanizing than a singles bar. Terry, a twenty-eight-year-old computer programmer with an aerospace company in California, is a case in point. At this time in her life she wants her sex strictly unencumbered and un-complicated. "I've always considered myself lucky to be working in a field that is predominately male. I'm young, unattached, and I enjoy sex. So why should I tie myself down? I've dated four or five of the guys I work with—more, if you count the ones from other departments—and I've had no problems. I haven't gotten serious with any one man and they seem to like it this way. There is always a sexual buzz going around the office. I kid around a lot, but I've made one rule—no dating or kidding with the boss. I've seen that lead to trouble too many times for other women. Dating co-workers is fine, but dating the boss can mess up your life. People think you are bucking for a raise or a promotion, your credibility goes out the window, and you lose your friends. It's just not worth it.

"One guy was put in over a group of us as a project supervisor after I had gone out with him a few times. I just stopped seeing him. At first he kept asking me out, until I finally told him why I was turning him down. At least that way he knew it wasn't personal. I guess you could say it was professional.''

In Terry's eyes and, apparently, to the other people in her office, her actions are perfectly acceptable—nothing to cause problems for anyone. But in less liberal environments, the serious flirt can create considerable trouble in an office, especially among the male employees. Most men still equate their masculinity with sexual prowess, and a woman who plays the field leaves a lot of hurt egos cringing behind her. For a man, working with a man who is all too obviously sleeping with the same woman you slept with just last month can be difficult, creating hard feelings and jealousy that sabotage the cooperation required in most offices.

Male flirts are just as deadly and can have the same unsettling effect among the women in an office. Wally is one of only a handful of bachelors in a largely female social services agency. Flirting to him is second only to breathing, and while most of the older women accept his compliments and attentions with an understanding that they mean little, the younger (and mostly single) ones are much more vulnerable. Several women felt he was giving them overt sexual signals, and it didn't help matters when he socialized with these women outside of the office and referred to the events as ''dates.'' The conversation almost always turned to sex. In truth he was sleeping with only one of the women (on a friendly basis, he insisted). But when the agency sent several of the employees to a statewide convention in a city ninety miles away, four different women colleagues, one of them married, showed up at his hotel room door in the evening, expecting to consummate their ''friendship.''

In some cases, the Terrys and Wallys of our world

are driven by something more than a simple desire for fun. In a 1982 interview in *The New York Times,* sociologists Philip Blumstein and Pepper Schwartz talked about one myth that seems to keep some people moving from one relationship to another. The idea that "the grass is always greener" is according to Blumstein, one of the most destructive myths promoted by the media and advertisers. "They make everything look so good. You can have the ideal man or woman, keep romance in your life, make everything better and more wonderful. Since real life in these times is tough, romantic fantasies have a great appeal. Unfortunately, they just skim the surface of what a relationship is really like."

For people who accept the myth, moving on to the next person quickly is fine, for a while at least. It makes life constantly exciting, if a bit hectic and unpredictable. The problem comes when the dance eventually ends, and the sexual gadabout is left with no real commitment, and no real relationship.

When a fling motivated by the desire for excitement turns into an affair, excitement can still be its driving force. Such relationships—which are really affairs of the genitals, not of the hearts—present no problems until passions cool and eyes start to wander. Even then, a clean break can head off trouble, with the lovers going their separate ways, trailing few regrets and a string of good memories. The only problem with this happy scenario is that people, being the perverse creatures they are, seldom cool down at the same rate. Even worse, one may decide that he or she really wants a love affair as well as a sexual affair. This means trouble.

One romance we heard about—a dream that turned into a nightmare for the woman involved—literally started with a dream. Joan is a statistician employed by a firm that produces annual reports, brochures, and sales material for other companies. She had worked with Alex, a commercial artist who specializes in the design of charts and graphs, for three years without incident until one night. Joan laughed ruefully as she told us about it:

"Alex was a nice guy, ten years older than I am, married, and just average looking. Certainly nothing to get excited about. We laughed and kidded at work but I never even had lunch with him. Then, one night, I had this incredible dream. It was romantic and so sexy. I had one of the most tremendous orgasms I've ever felt. When I woke up, I felt fantastic, and still sexy as hell. I couldn't wait to get to the office. I just wanted to see Alex, and touch him. By the time I got dressed and on the bus to work, I started to think how insane it was to carry the dream into reality, but I couldn't shake the feeling I had.

"Well, I walked straight in to see him as soon as I got to the office. He said 'Hi,' I said 'Hi,' just as we always did. But, God, he was sexy looking. For the rest of the day I found reasons to see him, even to move in close and lean on his shoulder. By the time I got home that night I was so excited, he became my fantasy lover.

"I didn't think I was that obvious, but within a week we were touching every chance we got, and a few nights later he asked me to have a drink after work. I found he usually stayed in town late at least one night a week to catch up on his freelance work. That became our night. The sex was great. Maybe not up to the dream, but for almost a year we clicked in bed like we had invented sex."

Joan freely admitted she wasn't in love with Alex. In fact, their affair started downhill when he began to talk about wanting to be with her more, and finally about getting a divorce and marrying her. That, according to Joan, was when the fun went out of the relationship. All she wanted Alex for was sex, an idea he found hard to handle. After they broke up, things were sticky at work for a while, but then they got back to predream normality. Joan recently met and married another man and told us she is very happy. Does she still have sexy dreams? Only about her husband, or so she says.

Joan didn't see herself as a home-breaker. All she wanted was a weekly roll in the hay. Unfortunately, many women, who like Joan start an affair with a married man specifically because they don't want any emotional involvement, end up with trouble when the man decides it's love. The woman feels guilty about hurting the man if she decides to stop seeing him or guilty about creating problems in his marriage if she doesn't. The second worry is usually undeserved. Most marriage counselors agree with Herbert Stearn, author of *The Extramarital Affair,* that "while affairs pose a threat to any marriage, they are usually the result of a troubled marriage, not the cause." A person who is wholeheartedly devoted to his spouse," Stearn wrote, "is not likely to get involved in a long-term affair."

But even when a long-term extramarital affair does develop, the odds against a divorce and remarriage are high. In most cases the already-married man or woman likes both the excitement of the affair and the security of marriage; and often, as was the case with Joan, the unmarried person has no desire to marry her or his lover. What we need, in the interest of greater harmony all around, is a litmus test for potential lovers, a way to identify and match up excitement seekers who aren't really looking, deep in their secret hearts, for commitment. This seems the only way to guarantee the expected fun and excitement without creating problems in the office and risking broken hearts and homes farther down the line.

THREE

POWER AND PASSION, 9 TO 5

3

THE DESIRE FOR POWER is the most complex, most fascinating, and most potentially damaging of the motives that lead to sexual liaisons in the office. People looking for love and excitement seldom create as many problems because their relationships don't threaten their co-workers' job opportunities or moral sensibilities, as the relationships of power seekers do.

Whether you believe that power is the ultimate aphrodisiac or consider it an evil, to be called powerful is almost always a compliment in the business community—one that ambitious people strive for. Using sex to get power is as old as Cleopatra and as new as what's-his-name down the hall. Sex as stepping-stone can be as simple and short-lived as flirting around the photocopy machine, or as established and long-lasting (at least in theory) as marrying the boss's daughter.

You'll usually find at least one corporate Lothario and office vamp in every organization. They are well known to their co-workers and are pointed out to newcomers with a certain amount of pride: "Watch out for Dick. He'll charm the pants off you," is the friendly warning given to a new woman. Or, for new men on the job, "Don't take Jane's come-on too seriously. She's just a tease, but a lot of fun."

Sometimes the comments are less friendly and are put-downs rather than half-joking cautions. Some varieties of flirt, male or female, are unpopular with their own sex, a feeling that can easily transfer to the flirtee.

Taking a flirt too seriously can lower your stock in the office, particularly if you have been warned. Despite these dangers, dedicated flirts are willing to be kidded, even disliked, because they see their actions as advantageous to themselves and harmless to others. One bright young woman who was quite aware of her reputation in the office says frankly that she flirts because it helps her learn more and get more interesting work to do. Gadding about the office, sweet-talking the men, she was asked to help out on projects that she would otherwise never even hear about.

Brenda is hiding a long-range plan under her flirting exterior. She doesn't intend to stay where she works—a large Wall Street brokerage house—for more than two years, and in this time she wants to work with as many people as she can to gain a broad understanding of the entire operation. She hopes eventually to become a broker in a smaller house, so the more she can learn now about how contacts are made and customers are handled, the better off she is.

Brenda's flirting involves more than sexual titillation. She is always willing to pitch in and help. She believes strongly that if she limited herself to the duties outlined in her job description, she would be just another young trainee to the rest of the staff. To move beyond that, she has found, requires more than friendliness and hard work. A bit of flirting helps.

She denies vigorously that what she does hurts herself or anyone else. Brenda's rules are simple: flatter men, help everyone, learn a lot, and move on. But there are also some no-no's: no dating, no drinks after work, no laying on of hands. She plays a strictly verbal game. She has found that the more men she flatters and flirts with, the safer she is from any serious involvement, something she definitely wants to avoid right now.

Brenda has been at the firm for eight months—in her first full-time job—and feels her game plan is working. As she says, "I may be their cute little pet, but I have access to a lot of informal training and information that other women who've been there for years don't. When I leave, I'll take that with me, but I mean to leave my flea collar behind."

Male flirting can be just as physically innocuous. A salesman for a large lithographic firm, whose charm is widely known and commented on, claims: "Sure, I turn on the sex appeal. That's what gets me past the secretaries to their bosses. They tell me lots of useful things about the company: when is a good time to see the boss; what kind of mood he is in; who is on his hit list that week. I don't make sexual passes—just kid and compliment a lot. I'm a firm believer in the spoonful-of-sugar theory.

"I don't take women out for lunch or drinks to gain information. I just rely on cheering them up in the office. The more I do this, the more they like me, and there are no messy complications. My wife wouldn't like it, and, frankly, neither would I."

Dick is a very successful salesman and is surprisingly well liked by both men and women in his company. He has a natural charm and uses it to the hilt. His father, he says, was a southern gentleman who raised him to treat women with respect and admiration. The fact that this works for him in a business way is no great surprise to him. "Everyone likes to be flattered. If more men understood this, they'd find the job a lot easier, and a lot more profitable."

Neither Brenda nor Dick feels there is anything wrong or personally demeaning in what they are doing. Both say they can drop the flirtatious role any time they want—meaning any time it stops working.

They do not concentrate on any one person for long,

and their flirting is generally designed to create an atmosphere of congeniality that will advance their careers.

Whereas Brenda and Dick are verbal flirts, other flirts use their bodies as well. Most of them are women, but there are men who have discovered that tight jeans can do a lot to get someone's attention. One extremely attractive and talented writer we'll call Jean always dresses in a quiet but sexy manner when she knows her editor is working on a story she has submitted. "I wear a soft blouse with a strategic button unbuttoned. He's a real breast man. He has never made a pass, but when I'm dressed like this, he seems to do less editing. I can't say I've done a scientific study, but, by God, things just seem to go along more smoothly when he has something other than words to look at and think about. I think I may even be helping the other staff writers. I add something to his day and put him in a good mood. I may be using my sex, but it is for a good cause—my ego."

Jean directs her attention chiefly at one man, not so much for career advancement as for personal satisfaction. She is proud of her work and, like most writers, feels that editors too often use a heavy hand. Directing her editor's attention from her copy to her body keeps the copy relatively unscathed without endangering Karen. This is good for her and, she insists, helps the rest of the staff, too.

These are three examples of rather mild power plays using flirtation, the kind that usually doesn't arouse the wrath of fellow workers the way more sexually aggressive maneuvering does. Flirting of this type is usually directed at some powerful person in the office, perhaps the boss himself (or herself; still a rare occurrence, but coming up fast). Flirting with the boss, and having him respond in a playful, approving way makes the women who use this technique feel special, somehow singled out from the rest of the staff. If matters stop there, nobody much cares and nobody gets hurt.

Too often, unfortunately, if the original overtures are mildly encouraged, the flirting becomes more strident and outrageous in an attempt to gain more attention, producing one of two unfortunate results. Either the boss—who is embarrassed or just tired of the game—slaps the flirt down hard; or the flirter finds it prudent to call a halt because the boss is taking matters too seriously. Either way the flirter's ego and job prospects are both bound to be hurt.

Flirting can be used in other ways to increase a person's visibility, a step that is particularly important to newcomers who want to stand out from the crowd. Staying late at the office to chat with someone higher up in the company is one good approach, especially if you take the trouble to learn what the other person's hobbies or interests are, and talk to him or her about them. This should be done subtly, of course, but most people love to chat about something they know well.

An advertising space buyer told us she found out that her boss's manager had wanted to be an actor when he was younger, and considered himself an authority on musical comedies. After boning up on the subject, she walked into his office one evening after work—she had met him briefly a week earlier at the office Christmas party—and asked him what he thought of a musical that had just been revived on Broadway; she was thinking of buying tickets. He told her, in detail, why it was no good, and advised her to see another, Off-Broadway revue.

She saw the show, liked it, and thanked him. From then on she stopped by his office occasionally to chat, at first about Broadway shows and then about more general subjects. This friendliness did not go unnoticed. Her boss took more interest in her work and she was asked to lunch by other men and women in the office. Visibility was her goal, and being seen talking to the top man—and having him call her by her first name—achieved it.

Visibility can develop without any special planning if you seize opportunities that occur naturally. Having the right connections, for example—through parents, schools, or even riding the right bus or train—can lead to meetings with higher-ups in a relaxed atmosphere in which a newcomer can make a good impression. Some discreet flirting in these situations can open doors to special opportunities, confidential information, and even promotions.

The office party is another prime chance for judicious flirting, as are company sales meetings, particularly ones held away from the office. Take men or women out from behind their usual desks, put them in their best dress-up clothes or an attractive tennis outfit, and "work" is a whole new game. If they are good at the game—flirting, not tennis—they are well on their way to making that all-important move from being just one of the crowd.

Naturally enough, the best flirts are the least obvious; they know that executives use social occasions to size up the staff informally. So successful people flirt discreetly and quietly. They want to be talked to, not talked about, later on.

Flirting often leads to dating, and someone who has been flirting to satisfy power needs usually ends up dating for the same reason. Whether or not dating includes sexual intimacy, it is a nonexclusive arrangement that occasionally leads to the more serious involvement of an affair. The most obvious power-inspired type of dating is with the boss or someone else higher-placed in the corporate structure, and it can open doors to the inner circle and make the dater privy to useful information for getting ahead in the job or moving on to a better one. Getting one's name and face known by the higher-ups is an important step, particularly for women, who seldom have direct access to the old-boy network that can ease a man's way up the ladder. One woman—we'll call her Donna— tells how judicially planned dating helped her make the career change she was after.

Donna was working as assistant to the personnel manager of the paper products division of a large conglomerate in the Midwest when she heard that the parent company was about to buy a small concern on the West Coast and considerably expand its operations. She learned of the projected purchase from one of the financial vice presidents, a man she had dated casually a few times. Donna had always wanted to live in California as well as move up in the company and decided this was her chance.

She deliberately became more involved (sexually and socially) with the vice president, who started bringing her to company affairs and to parties given by his friends within the corporation. There she met and talked to other high management people, men she hoped would remember her favorably when the time came. Donna never mentioned her interest in the West Coast until the company formally announced the purchase. Then she wrote to a number of the corporate officials she had met, expressing her interest in the new division and spelling out her knowledge of the company's health coverage, retirement plan, and other benefits. She pointed out how this knowledge would help make for a smooth takeover.

Donna received interviews with three of the five men she wrote to and was eventually assigned to handle liaison between the personnel departments of the parent company and the new West Coast division. She did a fine job and within a year she was named personnel manager of the division. All the while, Donna kept in touch with the vice president who had helped her along. She thanked him for his efforts, flattered him, and left him feeling good about himself and her.

Donna does not feel that she connived her way to the top; she simply used the best route open to her to get the chance she needed to prove herself. "If I had been a man," she says, "I might have played golf with the big-wigs, or kept my ears open in the men's room. But since I'm an attractive woman, I used that asset instead."

Most of the examples we have cited have involved women using sex or sexuality in one way or another to gain power from men. But it is far from a one-way street, particularly as more women gain positions that give them power to dispense or share. In one case we heard of, the power was social rather than business-oriented, but it was just as useful to the man involved, a young lawyer who worked for a large foundation.

Charles started dating a woman who worked in the foundation's grant division when he learned about her connections in the entertainment business. They dated strictly as friends, an arrangement that offered something to both of them. She wanted an intelligent, present-able escort for the steady round of parties and charitable events she attended with her friends in television and the theater; he had always been interested in show business and, now that he had his law degree, wanted to get into the legal and contractual end of the business.

Things worked out as Charles had hoped. He quickly became conversant with the workings of the entertain-ment business and was ready with the right names and terminology when his opportunity came—a dinner party at which he sat near an executive in one of the country's largest talent agencies. The man was impressed with Charles's knowledge, and when Charles said he was interested in making a move, the executive arranged for him to meet with other members of the agency. When a position opened in the contracts department a few months later, Charles got the job. He and the woman still date occasionally, still strictly as friends.

Dating as a way of getting more power, prestige or success isn't confined to co-workers, of course. Both men and women often "date" clients to land a sale or get a contract. Sex can be part of the bargain, subtly or not so subtly condoned by management. The boss's parting advice, "Be nice to him," can be a shorthand way of saying "Sleep with him if you have to, but get the contract."

How much of this is standard practice today is uncertain. There are plenty of stories, but most of them told in the third person—never about oneself or one's own company. One story we heard several times supposedly came out during a meeting with a group of advertising saleswomen, at which they all admitted having slept with clients to get or keep accounts. We wonder whether anyone would have thought of asking a group of salesmen the same question, and what their answer would have been. Eagerness to make a sale, and willingness to go an extra step to cinch it, is an equal opportunity trait.

Regardless of the ethics or morals involved, sleeping with a client can backfire financially if the boss disapproves of such shenanigans, officially or otherwise. And some clients are willing to accept the sex but think less of you and your company when the glow has faded. Not sleeping with a client is less likely to backfire, even if your company goes along with the idea. You have at least lived up to your convictions—a trait most people admire.

If you are called on the carpet for not complying, remember that under the new Equal Employment Opportunities Commission guidelines on sexual harassment, any boss who pressures employees to have sex with a client is asking for trouble.

The kind of power someone hopes to gain by going out with the right person or persons is not always so direct. It is often more a matter of self esteem than of power per se—a desire to feel more important, be noticed, be seen as more feminine (or masculine), or simply seem more exciting. These characteristics don't necessarily lead to more money or a better job, but they can make a job seem more valuable and interesting.

Dating the office beauty is a favorite ploy of the man who wants to show his boss and his co-workers how macho he is. It may even work. Several studies have shown that when a man is seen with a woman considered more attractive than he is, people judge him as more successful and smarter than they did before. The reasoning goes something like this: "He must have more to offer than I thought. How else could he get such a beauty?" Beautiful or not, many women also like being seen with important people. Dating the boss offers reflected glory, something to lord over their fellow workers, and is also a confidence builder. It helps place individuals, whatever their job, in the limelight, or at least get them out of the dark corners.

Sexual flings—short-term, hotly paced interludes— are another ploy in the quest for power. A young graduate student admits frankly that she slept with every member of her dissertation committee to make sure her doctoral thesis received a friendly reception. This buckshot approach has its adherents, but in many cases a single fling can do the trick, providing the flingee is the right person, the timing is good, and the fling is played out in an atmosphere of sophistication and savvy. If the memory is still fresh and pleasant, it's hard for a boss not to see a former bed partner in a favorable light when time for a promotion or raise comes around.

The next step on the power scale after dating or having a fling is an affair, which we define as an exclusive, sometimes long-term sexual relationship. It can involve living together, but this usually implies more commitment than is involved in an affair. The affair is the ultimate sex-to-gain-power ploy in the office; since it is more intense and continuous than flirting, dating, or a fling, and it presents more opportunities for getting and using power.

The affair involves ego, ambition, and a certain amount of callousness. Affairs are usually serious entanglements—fairly easy to begin, more difficult to continue, and usually very difficult to break off. Too often, when an affair ends, someone has been hurt, either personally or on the job. It is usually the woman who pays—but not always.

In the mid–1950s, long before we thought of writing about sex in the office, one of us (Pat) observed a case in which everyone lost out. The cast included an account executive for one of the top New York public relations firms; his private secretary; the mighty Eastern Railroad Association; and the equally powerful American Trucking Association.

The scenario: The account executive and his secretary had been having an affair, during which he promised her a promotion. Time passed, passion cooled, and the promised promotion was forgotten, by him at least. Sonya was a woman scorned, and her revenge was sweet. She quit, but before leaving, she took from her files all copies of the reports, memos, and other papers pertaining to her boss's main client—the Eastern Railroad Association (ERA)—and their long-standing struggle with the American Trucking Association for supremacy in long and short hauling.

The memos were important because the public relations firm had pulled some maneuvers that damaged the image of the truckers in the public eye. Many of these actions were what we would, since Watergate, call dirty tricks. Sonya sent copies of the memos detailing the actions to officials in the Washington office of the American Trucking Association, who passed them on to one of their members—the Pennsylvania Trucking Association (PTA). The PTA thereupon filed suit against the Eastern Railroad Association.

The struggle between the two shipping organizations—what a *Fortune* Magazine article called "The Railroad Trucker Brawl"—ended with everyone losing something. We don't know what happened to the account manager, but Sonya apparently didn't gain anything but personal satisfaction. Her "don't get mad, get even" scheme obviously took some planning. As Moliere said, "A woman always has her revenge ready."

In this case, a sexual liaison based on the desire for power created problems for all concerned. But using an affair to get what they want does work for some of the people some of the time. And since people who deliberately use sex for power are not ordinarily in the market for true love, any outcome that increases their power is successful.

Some women try to use sex as a stepping-stone up the corporate ladder, conducting each affair with a successively higher official of the company. In every company there are stories of women who have slept their way to the top, or are in the process of doing so. But truthfully, most of these stories seem to be just that—stories, based on wish fulfillment or a desire to denigrate the accomplishments of someone high in the company.

When a power-motivated affair works as planned, the rewards can be varied: a promotion, a raise, or just easier working conditions. One of the other pluses associated with these affairs is the feeling of power they give the participant over others in the office, particularly when the affair is with the boss. Pillow talk can be a powerful weapon. In one of the nastiest cases we found, the woman involved—we'll call her Elizabeth—got more than a raise and a promotion. She also successfully eliminated future competition by becoming her boss's spy and reporting—exaggerating when advantageous—the shortcomings of her co-workers. Her particular targets were two other women in the department, both good workers and well-liked by the staff.

Elizabeth's hold over the boss was strong enough, she said, that he was willing to believe anything she said. Egged on by her, he constantly criticized and belittled the work of the other two women until they quit. Last we heard, the affair was still going on. Elizabeth is sitting firmly in the catbird seat and no one dares challenge her. The one hope of the staff is that the passion will cool and the boss will come to his senses. More than just the two jobs have been affected—the office, which once was a functioning, friendly place to work, has become a we-against-them operation in which performance has suffered. Because affairs for power often end up this way, with the power being misused, co-workers are quick to notice and quicker to comment on such power plays, and to stop them early if they can.

In the power-motivated affairs mentioned so far, someone always ended up hurt—sometimes a participant,

sometimes an innocent bystander. In one such relationship with a happier ending both the man and the woman
got what they wanted, and the affair ended on a friendly
note. The woman, now an associate professor of art history at an eastern college, explains:

"I had an affair, early in my teaching career, with a
much older man who was a visiting lecturer on campus.
I don't think I started the affair with the conscious idea of
furthering my career, but I *was* more interested in him as
an artist and a celebrity than as a man. Being seen with
him made me feel more important, more part of the upper
echelon than my job as a Teaching Assistant warranted.

"I do think his near-celebrity status was the main
attraction to me. On his part, I realize now, he liked having young women sit at his feet and idolize him. I was
just the one that filled the role that semester. I suppose
in a way we were using each other. I'm sure the art department people knew I was sleeping with him and I liked
that, although I never mentioned him to anyone in a romantic way.

"I'm not sorry about having the affair, nor about the
fact that it ended after a few months. I learned a lot about
art and taste from him. I guess I just grew up and stopped
hanging on every word he said. That really was the beginning of the end. Once I was no longer sitting at his feet
adoringly, he wasn't that interested in me, either, so we
just drifted apart.

"At the beginning, both of us had a need. I wanted
to be noticed and be part of a world I had no real way of
entering. He liked being admired and looked up to, especially by pretty young girls. Beyond that, though, I think
he really did like to teach young people. And I don't mean
only sexually, although that was part of our unspoken
bargain. I mean he liked watching me begin to understand

and appreciate art in new and exciting ways. As a matter of fact, he became a full-time professor just a few years later, an arrangement that I'm sure was very satisfying to him. Just think, whole classes sitting at his feet, new ones every year.''

In a sense this was a power-motivated affair—the young woman wanted prestige, the man wanted to bolster his self-image. But it was an egalitarian arrangement that worked, and no one was worse for the experience.

An affair that is entered into for purely power reasons has a well-thought-out plan behind it. A successful power relationship requires a smart, seasoned, and calculating person to carry it out. The idea behind the 1959 film *Room at the Top* is as current as ever, although most of the people who want power have become a little more sophisticated and less blatant in their techniques. But beneath the sophisticated facade, people using people is still what the game is all about.

So far, we have concentrated on how people use sex to gain power in the office: what they do, from playful flirting to serious affairs, and what the consequences are. But the use of sex for power, unpleasant as it can be at times, is not nearly as objectionable as using power for sex—the subject of our next chapter.

FOUR

SEXUAL HARASSMENT

4

POWER CAN BE USED to gain sexual favors in ways that are obviously coercive or subtly intimidating. Either way, it adds up to sexual harassment—which for years has been one of the most widely known and best kept secrets of the business world. Nearly everyone knew it went on, but few talked about it, at least for publication. Most men didn't care, and most women were either afraid to bring it up or figured there was something wrong with them that attracted such unwanted attention. Fortunately these attitudes are changing, and with the publicity have come new studies, new regulations, and new court decisions that provide help and guidance in fighting such harassment.

The size and scope of the problem was first brought to public view by a 1976 *Redbook* Magazine article based on a survey of their readers. Among the 9,000 women who answered the questionnaire, 9 out of 10 said they had been harassed by male co-workers or supervisors at some time during their working lives. In 1978, Lynn Farley's book, *The Sexual Shakedown,* further documented how serious and widespread the situation was and explored the attitudes men and women held about it.

Since then, other stories in the media, sociological and psychological studies, congressional hearings, and court cases have brought this deviant form of office sex to public attention. Appearing before the Senate Labor Subcommittee hearings in April 1981, J. Clay Smith, Jr., acting head of the Equal Employment Opportunities Commission (EEOC), testified that there had been a steady increase in the number of sex discrimination cases in the federal courts since the guidelines had been published in November 1980. ''My instincts tell me this [the cases we have heard about so far] may be just the tip of the iceberg.''

Some men have also been subjected to this type of harassment, but it is still overwhelmingly a problem for women. For this reason—and to avoid the awkwardness of constant she/he, her/him verbal constructions—we will discuss harassment almost exclusively from the female side, with the understanding that some of what we say applies to men as well.

Sexual harassment is costly both for its victims and the companies they work for. Women who reject such overtures may lose their jobs, miss out on promotions, get fewer pay raises, or find bad evaluations on their work records. The debilitating effects on their physical and mental health can only be guessed at. Women who don't object avoid these problems, at least temporarily; but they lose respect—their own and others'—which may cost them even more dearly in the long run.

The extent to which sexual harassment is costly for companies is hinted at in a recent, nationally publicized study of 23,000 federal employees done by the Merit System Protection Board (MSPB). Based on the MSPB findings, the Office of Budget and Management estimated that in the two years from May 1978 to May 1980, sexual harassment cost the federal government $189 million in terms of job turnover (hiring expense, training costs, individual and group productivity, and absenteeism). This figure is conservative and includes only civilian federal employees. For the total working force, the cost could run into billions. Economically speaking, then, sexual harassment is not to be snickered at, and from a management point of view, tolerating it seems a costly way to run a business. Perhaps these economic facts of life will produce greater corporate efforts to stop harassment than will humanitarian considerations.

Until that millennium, there are other bright spots in the picture: The 1980 guidelines from the EEOC have put the ball squarely in the corporate court. Sexual harassment is no longer the fault without a name, and companies are responsible for their employees' actions—and in some cases, for the actions of nonemployees, if they take place on company territory. The guidelines spell out what constitutes sexual harassment, name its legal consequences, and suggest what a company should do to forestall or stop such actions.

Harassment comes in many sizes and varieties. Some is unmistakable. "Stopping Sexual Harassment," a booklet published by the Labor Education and Research Project in 1981, gave two blatant examples: "Lori Lodinsky, a military policeperson at Ft. Meade, was assigned to road duty on midnight shift. On her first night of training, her supervisor said he wanted to test her ability to maneuver a police sedan at high speed. 'He advised me to go real fast and weave in and out of the airstrip's flashing lights,' Lodinsky said. 'When I was going about 60 miles an hour, he started grabbing me all over my body.'

"Lodinsky did not report the attack, but after many other incidents, she applied for a discharge. She got a 'Chapter 5 Discharge—Unable to Cope with Military Life.' "

The second example is a civilian who was also discharged, in this case "for refusing to sleep with her boss on a business trip. Testifying at hearings on sexual harassment held in Detroit in May 1979, Maxine Munford said: 'My boss told me, ''You're going to have to get it through your head; you're going to screw me or lose your job.'' ' Munford lost her case because the judge doubted her credibility.''

Few would doubt that these were cases of harassment. But when it occurs at a less obvious level, what constitutes sexual harassment? Lawrence Vickery, general director of employment relations for the General Motors Corporation (GM), told us about ''a rough measure'' they use at GM. ''We ask, 'Would you be embarrassed to see your remarks or behavior displayed in the newpaper or described to your family?' That really brings it home and makes everyone think.''

The people who answered the MSPB federal study mentioned earlier agreed strongly about one thing when it came to harassment: what a superior said or did to a subordinate was much more likely to be thought of as harassment than similar words or actions coming from an equal. Beyond this, the definition of sexual harassment has proved to be a problem for researchers, pollsters, and management, as well as for employees themselves.

In the MSPB study, for example, 42 percent of the women employees and 15 percent of the men said they had been sexually harassed on the job during the previous two years. They were then asked which forms of uninvited behavior they considered to be sexual harassment ''if it happened to you or someone else at work.'' The most severe form, of course, was rape or attempted rape, which was reported by about 1 percent of the women who answered the survey. Based on this, Ruth Prokop, then chairperson of the MSPB, estimated that at least 9,000 women working for the federal government had been subjected to rape or attempted rape.

Aside from rape, the actions women described as

most harassing were letters, phone calls, or other material of a sexual nature, pressure for sexual favors, and touching, leaning over, cornering, or pinching. Pressure for dates, sexually suggestive looks or gestures, and sexual teasing, jokes, or remarks were considered less severe.

These were the overall findings of the study. There was a difference between the sexes on which of these actions were considered harassing. Men and women agreed, almost unanimously, that most of the actions listed above, from rape through touching and pinching, should be considered harassment. But men were less sure about sexual looks and comments, especially when they were done by a co-worker rather than a supervisor.

Other major findings of the federal study include the following:

- Harassers frequently bother more than one person, and the incidents reoccur over an extended period of time.

- Most federal employees who have worked in private business feel harassment is the same in both sectors.

- Victims say that direct, personal action, such as being assertive, is the best way to stop unwanted attention.

- Few victims report harassment through formal channels, but those who do find it helpful.

- A sizable number of employees say they have left jobs because of the unwanted attention.

- Harassment has a more negative effect on personal well-being and morale than it does on individual productivity or group performance.

- Most employees, including supervisors, are either unaware of the formal remedies that are available or are skeptical about their effectiveness.

- Despite this, most people who have suffered from sexual harassment feel that management can reduce the problem considerably if it really wants to.

The MSPB survey was conducted among a random selection of federal employees—workers and supervisors alike. Its main purpose was not only to learn how much harassment was going on but to make managers and workers aware of the problem and of the options open to people who were being harassed. Another survey, this one conducted by *Redbook* Magazine and the *Harvard Business Review* in 1981, was aimed at middle and upper management echelons. It concentrated on what they considered harassment, how much harassment they felt occurred in their organizations, what the company policy toward it was, what they would like it to be, and how they themselves had felt if or when they had been harassed. The study included both typical vignettes and direct questions about harassment and produced these conclusions:

- Most of the managers believed that harassment was a serious matter. Ten percent said they knew of cases in which a supervisor had given a poor evaluation to a subordinate who had refused sexual favors.

- Both men and women saw harassment as a power issue.

- Both sexes agreed on what harassment is but disagreed on how often it occurred. Asked whether the issue was "greatly exaggerated," less than half of the women managers agreed, compared to two-thirds of the men.

- Top management was least aware of sexual harassment as a problem, followed by middle management; lower-level management was most aware.

- Most of the managers (73 percent) favored company policies against sexual harassment, but only a few of their companies (29 percent) had such formal policies.

- Most managers of both sexes saw the EEOC guidelines as necessary and reasonable. The provisions dealing with dirty jokes and sexual innuendo were considered hardest to prove, making these areas toughest to control. These are also, unfortunately, the most prevalent kind of harassment—the kind nearly all women have experienced on occasion; it is the most difficult for them to handle because it is the most tolerated—even condoned—by other people in the office.

Despite the difference in the emphasis of the two studies and the people involved—one was aimed at labor, the other at management—their findings coincided in many ways. Both groups agreed that most companies lack a company policy toward harassment and that most workers don't know what to do if they feel they have been harassed.

If you were to draw up a profile of the person most likely to be harassed, based on these and other studies, it would start with these characteristics: young, unmarried, female, attractive, working in a low-paying, low-status job. But like all profiles, this is merely an outline, hiding within it women (and some men) of all ages, job classifications, and marital conditions. In the federal study, the sexual composition of the particular office influenced the likelihood of harassment: the higher the percentage of men, the more harassment of women. Job dependency also influenced harassment: if someone really needed a job, the amount and severity of harassment increased.

A somewhat clearer profile of harassers emerges from the studies. Usually they are men, older than their victims (a recent court decision awarded $13,000 each to two young women who had been harassed by their seventy-three-year-old boss). They are often in a supervisory position, married, and considered unattractive by the victims.

Lawrence Vickery, the GM executive mentioned earlier, has some unofficial ideas of his own about potential harassers and how to handle them. "In my opinion," he told us, "probably less than five percent of the total male work force is even capable of doing anything like sexual harassment. The other 95 percent might have it on their minds but would never do it. Too many constraints are operating on them—from wife, church, family—that whole moral rigidity. But the other five percent can be dealt with very easily. You know who they are because you see them operating.

"All you have to do with those fellows is call them into your office, close the door, and say, 'I want to talk to you about sexual harassment. Don't say a word—I'm telling you that I suspect you might be guilty of doing some of these things. I want you to know that it has got to stop. I'm going to be watching you, everyone will be watching you. And if it doesn't stop, then you're a dead duck.' "

The federal study made some additional points about the differences between male and female harassers. Men were much more likely than women to suffer homosexual advances—22 percent of the men who had been harassed said it had been done by a man or men, compared to only 3 percent of the women who had been bothered by women. Men who harass women are generally older than their victims, while women who harass men are younger. Most male harassers are married, while most female harassers are divorced or single. Harassment of both sexes is done most often by co-workers—after all, there are many more of them than there are supervisors, but a larger percentage of women than men report harassment by supervisors.

These statistics tell us something about the demographics of harassment, but the reasons for it are more speculative. Psychologists generally point to three motives: The simplest is sexual desire—lust looking to be satisfied. The second is personal power. A boss harasses a woman working for him to make himself feel more important, more virile, more in control of his domain. The third motive is social control. Harassment is a safe weapon for the supervisor who doesn't really want to hire or promote women. Since he can't do this legally, he can use his authority to embarrass or humiliate them and perhaps even get them to quit. Even if this doesn't happen, he has "put them in their place." These three motives are not as distinct in real life as they are on paper. Most cases of harassment involve more than one motive, and some are impelled by all three.

Sexual harassment by a boss or supervisor harkens back, in a way, to the medieval practice of *droit du seigneur,* which gave the feudal lord the right to sleep the first night with the bride of any of his vassals. Although feudalism ended many centuries ago, some people still feel that to be a boss is to be at least semidivinely ordained—to have certain inalienable rights. The power to hire, fire, and give raises is misappropriated by these petty tyrants and used for their own purposes, sexual and otherwise.

The idea of using a paycheck as a license for sex seems ludicrous, if not sick, but it happens all the time. Men who would never think, or at least never follow through on, the idea of pinching a woman's breast in a bus or on the street, feel free to subject their secretary to this humiliation as if it were a job-given right. This kind of power-based harassment is not limited to less-educated, lower-echelon supervisors. Doctors, lawyers, government officials, professors, and high-ranking business executives have all been guilty of it at different times.

Some companies use the ambiguity of current EEOC guidelines as an excuse to delay issuing specific company regulations against sexual harassment. The director of personnel planning at a major financial company cited this uncertainty. (He asked us not to identify his company, which, he said, was still working on its program.) "What we've done so far," he said, "is issue a one-page memo to all managers saying that harassment is still an area of ambiguity, even though we know that this unattractive type of behavior goes on. I also threw in other types of harassment—racial slurs, ethnic jokes, that kind of thing. Now if Washington ever decides exactly what sexual harassment is, we will come out with a more formal policy."

The use and abuse of power is an element that underlies much sexual harassment, but there are other factors, particularly when the unwanted attention comes from a co-worker rather than a boss. Sometimes it stems from the locker-room machismo belief that any woman is fair game. Other harassment springs from the fear that women will take over men's jobs, and the need to punish them for their presumption. Men who feel emotionally threatened by the idea that ambitious women are defying their traditional roles of wife and mother may use sexual aggressiveness in the same humiliating way. Whatever the motive, the result is the same: ugly, unwanted harassment.

For someone who is being harassed, the motives of the harasser usually don't matter; the important point is how to handle the situation. Organizations and individuals who work with the problem of harassment regularly offer these suggestions: To start with the most obvious, if you have been the victim of rape, or attempted rape, call the police. There is no other reasonable way to deal with this crime, whatever the motive.

Less violent attacks call for other kinds of direct action. The hardest problem for most women to handle is harassment by the boss. When it is clear that acquiescing to sexual demands means job enhancement and that refusing means job diminishment (you might call this the carrot-and-stick approach to harassment) the experts advise this sequence of steps:

1. Tell the man causing the trouble exactly how you feel about what he is doing.

2. Write your objections to his behavior in a letter and give it to him. Keep a copy and, if possible, arrange to have a third person witness that he receives the letter. Labor economist and mediator Mary P. Rowe suggests the following formula for writing the letter: First, state the problem clearly, in as detailed and factual a way as you can. Second, describe the actions you object to and how they make you feel. Third, say what you would like to have happen next: what the other person should do or not do. Usually this is just

stopping certain actions, but if he has taken some punitive action against you, say precisely what it is and how it can be rectified.

This kind of letter serves at least three purposes. It may be enough in itself to stop the objectionable behavior. It also helps you face the problem, realize it isn't your fault, and feel better about yourself because you have acted to correct the situation. If the harassment doesn't stop, and you feel it necessary to take further action, the letter serves both as evidence and as an indication to management and the courts that you tried to solve the problem before getting others involved. If you decide to go further and file a civil rights case, document as many incidents of harassment as you can, involving you and other women (studies show that harassers usually don't stop with just one woman). Write down all the details—time, place, specific words and actions—and ask any witnesses to do the same. Follow the same approach if you decide to complain through whatever channels are available to you within your company—a union, personnel department, other supervisors.

Many employees are not aware what formal complaint channels are open to them, and many who are aware are loathe to use them for fear of retaliation. This fear is often legitimate, regardless of what complaint procedures have been formally established, if top management doesn't have a strong commitment to following through—that is, first making sure that complaints are investigated thoroughly and corrective action taken, if the complaints are justified; and second, seeing that no punitive action is taken against the complainant by the harasser or his friends. This happens all too often, which is why many women either quit a job rather than complain or decide to put up with the harassment.

When it comes to purely vocal harassment, such as dirty jokes or sexual innuendos, women often find themselves caught in a bind. They are damned if they assert themselves and openly show their displeasure, by being labeled as either bitchy or prudish. If they remain silent and try not to show their annoyance, their damnation comes in the form of an increase in the distasteful behavior.

Most experts advise women to deal with this situation directly and immediately. A firm but friendly ''I don't like that joke (remark, picture)'' can sometimes nip harassment in the bud. It puts even the most obtuse leerer on notice, right from the start, that you are not interested and are not leading him on in some subtle way. If this doesn't do the trick, more direct action is needed.

Most women find it best to enlist the help of co-workers in stopping this kind of behavior. Vickery at GM backs this approach. ''Our recommendation for women is that they support and reinforce each other. If you see sexual harassment taking place, encourage the woman to come forward and tell her story. When women do that, the guy will usually leave them alone.''

Some women feel strong enough to assert themselves individually in a way that makes the offender look ridiculous by calling loud attention to his remarks or actions. This is a particularly tricky business when the offender is your superior; it takes a lot of guts to do what one secretary did to her boss, who constantly looked at her breasts rather than her face when he talked to her. One day, as he was doing this, she knelt down and addressed her answer to his crotch. He got the point.

The sarcastic touch can be helpful, as it was in this case, but it can easily backfire. Unless you are really sure of yourself and your target, a less flamboyant approach is recommended.

Explain calmly what you object to. If this doesn't work, you might try getting a copy of the EEOC guidelines against sexual harassment from your personnel office, circling the pertinent passages, and either posting them on the bulletin board or giving them directly to the offender.

As mentioned earlier, various kinds of behavior—jokes, looks, comments—fall into a grey area that some women and many men feel is not quite harassment. This is particularly true when the people involved have equal power and standing in the company. In this situation, certain actions may be seen as either pleasurable or offensive, depending on whether the attraction is mutual. If the woman takes offense, she usually feels free to speak up and stop the offensive behavior. (It's not always that easy, of course, but this direct approach should be tried before taking any further, more official action to stop harassment.)

Some companies have attacked this kind of harassment directly. One of them is Bank of America. According to Pat Taber, a vice president at the bank's corporate headquarters in San Francisco, the company's policy statement goes into "different types of harassment, like verbal harassment, jokes, slurs, derogatory comments, unwanted physical contact, repeated or blocking movement, interference with normal work, visual harassment, derogatory posters, cartoons, or drawings, unwanted sexual advances which condition employee benefits upon exchange of sexual favors. It is published in our standard personnel manual."

Bank of America trains its managers, Taber says, "to hold staff meetings and speak to the employees about our affirmative action program and equal opportunity employment, and part of that includes sexual harassment

—telling employees that of course they should step forward if they feel that harassment is occurring.''

When a boss does something that can be considered at all suggestive, the potential problem becomes much more serious. Even if he is not trying to coerce anyone—he is really socially and sexually interested and wants to be treated as a man, not as a boss—the overtone of harassment still exists. He *is* the boss, like it or not, and this authority transforms a normal social interaction into possible harassment. It may be hard on the man or even on the woman, but boss-subordinate relationships are the cause of most sex-based problems in the office.

There is another common type of subtle sexual putdown that can undermine careers and yet doesn't seem to fit under the EEOC guidelines. It often comes in the guise of an outwardly complimentary remark. At a meeting, for example, just before a woman gives a report, her boss or someone else at the meeting remarks how cute she is or what great legs she has—reducing her professional standing and making her a sexual object rather than a business associate. Precisely to avoid this type of putdown, many women deliberately project an ''iron maiden'' image in the office.

The EEOC guidelines are not laws, but they specify that any company that has fifteen employees or more can be held responsible for sexual harassment that occurs on its premises. The regulations offer a positive incentive as well as a threat for companies to stop harassment. If an employee sues a company under Title VII of the 1964 Civil Rights Act, or files a civil suit against it, the company that can show that it has complied with the guidelines and has set up a program to deal with harassment stands a better chance of winning the case.

Even people who know that there are new rules

against sexual harassment don't know exactly what they are. For this reason, we have reprinted the pertinent section of the guidelines.

Early court decisions against sexual harassment, filed under Title VII, were won primarily on tangible evidence that such harassment had cost the victims their jobs. In *Barnes* v. *Castle,* for example, Paulette Barnes charged that her job with the U.S. Environmental Protection Agency was abolished because she refused to engage in sexual relations with her boss. The U.S. District Court of Appeals in Washington, D.C., reversing an earlier decision, ruled that such harassment came under the protection of Title VII. Barnes settled out of court and was awarded $18,000 in back pay and legal fees.

Recently, however, this narrow definition of how Title VII applies to sexual harassment was expanded. The U.S. Court of Appeals reversed a decision of a district court (*Bundy* v. *Jackson*) that included in its opinion the statement: "The making of improper sexual advances to female employees [was] standard operating procedure, a fact of life, a normal condition of employment." Thus, the court concluded, the case did not violate the provisions of Title VII. In its ruling, the court of appeals stated that a woman did not have to prove that she had resisted sexual demands and/or that she had been penalized in some way for this refusal. In effect, the appeals court ruled that harassment, in itself, was a violation of Title VII. Employers are liable for sexual harassment because it creates an offensive "discriminatory environment" by "poisoning the atmosphere of employment."

This landmark decision will obviously make it easier to win court cases even when it is difficult to prove that sexual advances were refused or that such refusal subsequently was punished by firing, lack of advancement, or other discrimination. Harassment is no longer a natural condition of employment—"boys will be boys"—but a violation of civil rights.

In other areas, the body of law involving sexual harassment is still developing. Certain actions by a superior are clearly illegal, but the liability of an employer when the same words or actions involve a co-worker or someone other than an employee—a customer, a salesman, a delivery man—is still open to question.

Another section of the revised guidelines that has not been tested is the one that says an employer may be liable for sex discrimination against third parties who have been denied opportunities or benefits because another employee provided sexual favors to a person who supervised both of them.

The EEOC guidelines, like other affirmative action programs, have been attacked from many quarters—business leaders, the press, and even judges involved in Title VII cases. Similar comments were heard during the 1981 congressional hearings on harassment. During these, ERA opponent Phyllis Schlafly suggested that the way women walked was an indication of their moral character. This idea—that women "get what they ask for" from men at work—is the argument used most often when people defend behavior that others call harassment and deny the need for regulations against it.

Fortunately, most working men and women seem to consider the guidelines a boon. In the *Harvard Business Review/Redbook* survey, 57 percent of the men and women who hold management positions considered the guidelines both *reasonable* and *necessary,* while another 15 percent went further, calling them *highly reasonable* and *very necessary.* There were, admittedly, dissenters who felt the guidelines would make it more difficult—in some cases, impossible—for men and women to work together. One manager complained bitterly that for the guidelines to work, "women would have to be brought under a new and strict dress code."

The EEOC guidelines can help, but what really counts is organization policy and the commitment of top management to prevent or stop harassment. Formal statements defining harassment and spelling out the company's strong opposition to it; meetings; training sessions and sensitivity sessions with supervisors to discuss the subject; memos informing employees of grievance procedures—all help create a climate in which harassment is the frowned-upon exception rather than the accepted norm.

Whatever the motive for sexual involvement—power, love, or excitement—and whatever the method used—flirtation, an affair, long-term commitment, or sexual harassment—the office is a sexy place. As we discuss in the next chapter, it provides a powerful psychological environment for the feelings and emotions that lead to sex and romance.

Here is the text of the EEOC guidelines dealing with sexual harassment:

Part 1604—Guidelines on Discrimination Because of Sex
1604.11 Sexual Harassment

(a) Harassment on the basis of sex is a violation of Sec. 703 of Title VII. Unwelcome sexual advances, requests for sexual favors, and other verbal or physical conduct of a sexual nature constitute sexual harassment when (1) submission to such conduct is made either explicitly or implicitly a term or condition of an individual's employment, (2) submission to or rejection of such conduct by an individual is used as the basis for employment decisions affecting such individual, or (3) such conduct has the purpose or effect of unreasonably interfering with an individual's work performance or creating an intimidating, hostile, or offensive working environment.

(b) In determining whether alleged conduct constitutes sexual harassment, the Commission will look at the record as a whole and at the totality of the circumstances, such as the nature of the sexual advances and the context in which the alleged incidents occurred. The determination of the legality of a particular action will be made from the facts, on a case by case basis.

(c) Applying general Title VII principles, an employer, employment agency, joint apprenticeship committee or labor organization (hereinafter collectively referred to as ''employer'') is responsible for its acts and those of its agents and supervisory employees with respect to sexual harassment regardless of whether the specific acts complained of were authorized or even forbidden by the employer and regardless of whether the employer knew or should have known of their occurrence. The Commission will examine the circumstances of the particular employment relationship and the job functions performed by the individual in determining whether an individual acts in either a supervisory or agency capacity.

(d) With respect to conduct between fellow employees, an employer is responsible for acts of sexual harassment in the workplace where the employer (or its agents or supervisory employees) knows or should have known of the conduct, unless it can show that it took immediate and appropriate corrective action.

(e) An employer may also be responsible for the acts of nonemployees, with respect to sexual harassment of employees in the workplace, where the employer (or its agents or supervisory employees) knows or should have known of the conduct and fails to take immediate and appropriate corrective action. In reviewing these cases the Commission will consider the extent of the employer's control and any other legal responsibility which the employer may have with respect to the conduct of such nonemployees.

(f) Prevention is the best tool for the elimination of sexual harassment. An employer should take all steps necessary to prevent sexual harassment from occurring, such as affirmatively raising the subject, expressing strong disapproval, developing appropriate sanctions, informing employees of their right to raise and how to raise the issue of harassment under Title VII, and developing methods to sensitize all concerned.

(g) Other related practices: Where employment opportunities or benefits are granted because of an individual's submission to the employer's sexual advances or request for sexual favors, the employer may be held liable for unlawful sex discrimination against other persons who were qualified for but denied that employment opportunity or benefit.

FIVE

THE SENSUAL CORPORATION

5

I N RECENT YEARS, everyone from psychologists to environmentalists to writers of how-to-succeed-in-three-easy-lessons books have been pushing their theories on how office decor should be changed to make workers happier and, more important, more productive. But unless you've reached the upper corporate levels, your office surroundings are probably still either drab, cluttered, or both. Or, if changes have been made, your office is now high-tech spit and polish. Neither is a very promising environment for romance.

Why, then, do flirting, affairs, and sometimes plain old sex occur so regularly in rather dull places obviously set up to facilitate business transactions, not erotic interludes? The simplest reason echoes bank robber Willie Sutton's laconic reply to a reporter's question about why he robbed banks: "That's where the money is." Sex and romance develop in offices because that's where the people are. Men and women who meet under all kinds of emotional conditions for eight hours a day, five days a week, month after month, are likely to get together in ways not mentioned in the corporate policy manual.

Proximity is the word psychologists use to describe this prime ingredient in the sexual stew. Assuming you are basically compatible, the more you see and work with people, the greater chances are that you will like them and want to know them better. Clearly, familiarity does not normally breed contempt, then. Psychologist Robert Zajonc did a series of experiments on the effects of repeated exposure to others and found that familiarity almost always generates positive feelings. The converse, Zajonc says, is equally true: We feel uncomfortable and even threatened when faced with the unfamiliar.

Although the idea of a sexy stranger charging out of nowhere seems romantic, that's not the way it happens. Whether the driving force is mad passion or cool calculation, we usually fall in love with and marry a person we have been close to for years, not a romantic stranger glimpsed across a crowded room. This is borne out by sociologist A. C. Clarke, who surveyed couples applying for marriage licenses as to where they lived. He found that 37 percent lived within eight blocks of each other, and another 17 percent within sixteen blocks.

This is just one of many psychological and sociological studies of proximity, attraction, and other factors that help explain why the office breeds sex and romance. Most of the research was done outside the office, but the findings apply to work because an office is the world in microcosm. The same elements that bring us together and drive us apart in discos or on the beach affect us in the office. A study of apartment friendships done thirty years ago is a good example.

When psychologist Leon Festinger interviewed the occupants of a recently built apartment complex, he discovered that friendships developed much more often between next-door neighbors or those just a door away. This was not a small difference: the power of proximity was so great that people seldom described anyone who lived even five apartments away as a friend. Festinger also found that men and women who lived near the mailboxes, close to exits or entrances, or near the stairwells— in the flow of traffic, in other words—had considerably more friends than other, presumably just as nice people who lived elsewhere in the apartment complex.

Festinger's findings have an obvious application to offices. You are more likely to develop close relations, sexual or otherwise, with someone who works near you than you would with the same person if he or she worked around the corner or on the next floor. Similarly, men and women who work near where others congregate or pass by—the water cooler, the coffee machine, the rest rooms, along an open corridor—are exposed to people more frequently and are thus more likely to develop a relationship with them.

A designer named Phil learned personally a few years ago how important location is. When he first joined a newly formed architectural firm, his office was at the end of a corridor, behind the reception area. It was a big corner office with large windows—both desirable status symbols according to most observers of office power and protocol. But it had one big drawback: Phil was shut off from the flow of traffic, so no one ever passed his door accidentally or dropped in casually. People came to his office when they had something to see him about, but that was it. He missed out on the casual chitchat that would let him know what was happening in the company unofficially, which is how most really important and interesting things happen.

As the company grew and more people were hired, it became necessary to expand various departments. Phil was moved with the other senior designers to another floor. His new office was much smaller, had only one window, and was not nearly as luxurious. But he soon felt much more a part of the company than he had before. The mail slots, the bathrooms, and a back exit to the elevators were all down the hall from him, resulting in a constant stream of people past his office. Within a few weeks he had gotten to know more people—particularly those from the business side—than he had met in all his time downstairs. His office became a stopover for everyone from the receptionist to the company president.

One of the people Phil came to know was Susan, a bookkeeper who worked on the same floor. Although they rarely had any business dealings, they usually arrived at work about the same time, since both liked to get in early to get the day organized. Phil saw Sue every day as she went to get her mail, and she soon started stopping by to talk. This led to lunches, dinners, romance, and, eventually, marriage. Phil says, only half joking, "I owe my marriage to being moved to the right office."

When UCLA psychologist Albert Mehrabian studied the effects of different office arrangements, he found that the open office/bullpen setup was the most conducive to friendly relations. The lack of walls encouraged fellow workers to tell jokes, get together on common job problems, exchange the latest gossip, and—not least important —arrange lunch dates more easily. In short, people got to know and like each other better. And while Mehrabian did not ask about romance, the increased camaraderie and personal exchanges were bound to lead naturally to sexual entanglements.

Proximity, as this research shows, is a big boost to friendship and romance. It increases the chance that we will get to know someone well enough to desire a closer relationship. But what makes us like one person we live or work close to more than another who lives or works just as close? Research on romantic involvement shows that before we become sexually involved with someone (ignoring the one-night stand, which usually owes more to opportunity and alcohol than anything else), there is a definite pattern of behaviors that leads to intimacy.

The clearest statement of this idea is provided by psychologists George Levinger and L. Rowell Huesmann who set up a model of romantic involvement they call "incremental exchange theory." It includes a series of actions and reactions that, if each person responds positively, produces romance, sex, and possibly marriage. Here is their menu of behaviors:

1. meeting

2. request for date

3. dating

4. disclosure

5. romance

6. sex

7. harmony

8. future plans

9. commitment

10. permanence

11. proposal

Each of these steps requires a reciprocal reaction from the other person involved. If, particularly early in the game, one of them responds negatively, the romance could end right there. A vital early step is disclosure. When we are attracted to someone, it seems natural to tell them something personal about ourselves—an incident from our childhood, perhaps, or an embarrassing experience. If the other person reciprocates, a feeling of warmth and friendship is created.

Such personal revelations are encouraged by situations that occur naturally in response to many work environments: late hours, the after-work drink and resulting camaraderie, business trips. When two people find themselves working late in a nearly empty office, they tend to be less formal and more relaxed. Ties come off, feet go up on desks, they send out for food, and a bottle may come out of the bottom right drawer. Exhaustion can be as relaxing, or as exciting, as the situation dictates. Whichever happens, the result is a friendlier, warmer, closer-knit feeling than develops during the normal nine-to-five workday. The feeling naturally leads to discussion of families, friends, or other favorite things—in other words, mutual self-disclosure. A woman who previously thought her male colleague somewhat stuffy and patronizing now discovers he's really just a bit shy and has wanted to get to know her better for months. Or two people who haven't worked closely together before find out they have mutual interests in skiing or gardening or the theater.

Much the same thing happens when office friends become drinking buddies, or softball buddies, or bowling buddies—anything that brings them together in a relaxed after-work atmosphere. The camaraderie generated by the "let's unwind" drink after work produces the same stimulating, off-the-cuff friendliness as working late. And when the two situations are combined, as they often are, the push toward even greater intimacy is that much stronger. Sharing gripes, jokes, and stories leads to warmer personal feelings that can easily heat up into sexual feelings.

The situation that is the most tempting of all, the one most conducive to romance, is the business trip. Here two people are completely away from the office, geographically and emotionally. The usual script calls for frequent meals together and socializing with customers, also in tandem. This means conversation, more than ever before, and suddenly people who were always businesslike in the office are discussing favorite movies, their childhood, and even personal problems. They come to feel more for each other, to understand more about each other. This can lead to nothing more than a closer friendship. Or it can open a door to the bedroom.

One interesting aspect of the situations and feelings that lead to sex in the office is that seemingly contradictory causes can produce similar results. For example, two people who simply don't have enough to keep them busy on a late-night shift can find their own ways of making time pass pleasantly. The opposite situation—too much work, too much pressure—can be just as stimulating, as it was to a purchasing agent in the Midwest. Middle-aged and balding, he said that an affair with his young assistant started ''only after she and I had been working incredibly hard for several months. The company was moving its national headquarters to another state, and our office was responsible for the move.

''This meant catering to the whims and wishes of everyone from the chief executive officer to the mailroom boys. Every day someone changed his mind about what he needed and when he needed it. At first the job seemed like nothing but an endless, often infuriating grind. Gradually, our late nights together, which often ended with one or both of us laughing helplessly at another inane request, became fun. Ann kept me from blowing my stack a dozen times, and I realized I was actually looking forward to coming to work. It didn't take long for this feeling to change from liking her, to wanting to be with her, to needing to be with her. I asked her to have a drink, then dinner, and then there we were, in bed.

''It's funny. The glow began to wear off in a few

months, just about the time our workload returned to normal. Maybe we both needed that extra tension and excitement to keep things going.''

Just as boredom or overwork can lead to office romance, so can shared success or failure. The erotic power of success is easy to understand. Common sense supports the idea that when things are going well, everything and everybody looks better to us. It is also supported by numerous studies of what (other than sheer good looks) makes people attractive to us. Psychologist Donn Byrne's Law of Attraction, for example, is based on the simple Skinnerian principle of reinforcement: we like people who give us pleasure (positive reinforcement), and we dislike those who give us pain (negative reinforcement).

But Dr. Byrne carries his theory a step further. We also equate our feeling for people with what happens to us when they are around. We usually like people who are with us in good times and think less of those we connect with our misfortunes. Romance is especially likely if two people work together for a long time on a project that wins praise for both of them. A woman who works on the magazine a large insurance company publishes for its employees was asked to look into the feasibility of a new column that had been suggested—a series of short geographical or historical notes about different cities in which the company has offices. A young man who had recently joined the staff was assigned to help her out.

The job took several months, most of it in the office, on the phone, or looking through reference books to see if enough interesting information was available to make a continuing column feasible. Late hours became routine, especially as the deadline for the report drew near. Elaine tells the rest of the story:

''Dan and I felt the column idea would work, so we

decided to go for broke with a strongly favorable recommendation. It required a lot of work, and a lot of late hours, but we got our recommendation in on time. We were worried, but fortunately we didn't have to wait long. The editor approved the idea of the column, called both of us in to say what a fine job we'd done, and assigned the column to me, with a byline.

"I never thought of Dan in any romantic way when we first started to work together. I didn't know him very well—he had only joined the company a couple of months earlier—and anyway, he was at least five years younger than I am. But I enjoyed working with him, and we started stopping in for a drink after work. Even so, he was just a nice guy, nothing more than that. But the day we heard that the column was okayed, and that I would get a byline to write it, Dan insisted that we go out together to celebrate. We went to my place for a nightcap, one thing led to another, and he ended up sleeping over.

"That was six months ago. I still see him every now and then. The company is good, the sex is better, and the fact that neither of us wants to get serious makes everything that much nicer. I'm really glad we got to work together on the column idea. If we hadn't, I don't see how we would ever have gotten together."

Shared success like this is a wonderful catalyst to romance. But shared failure can be just as powerful. We all know the feeling. Suddenly, everything goes wrong. The project you have been working on for months has fallen through. Your boss has berated you in front of the staff, and your wife doesn't think much of you either, for a totally different reason. So you look around. You can't be certain, but it sure looks like some of those miserable people you've been covering up for all these years are enjoying your predicament. All of them, that is, except good old Meg, who you know was the boss's target last week. She's trying hard not to look at you with too much sympathy. But that's just what you need right now, a soft shoulder to cry on. She's there, she's been through the same wars; she seems to have a warm, loving glow about her. What better medicine than to wallow in your grief over a dry martini, preferably with Meg to hold your hand.

The thrill of victory. The agony of defeat. Either can lead to romance, particularly for the people that psychologist Marvin Zuckerman calls sensation-seekers—individuals for whom risk-taking is a normal way of life. They are more extraverted, more hedonistic, and more danger-loving than most. Their sports, for example, are more likely to be hang-gliding, skiing, or parachute jumping than golf or tennis—although they might also enjoy a spot of *apres-ski* bridge, if the stakes are high enough. At work, they are the men and women on the fast track—young achievers in the business world. They want it all, they want it now, and they are willing to risk everything on a big score.

When you bring two such people together in a situation where they are putting their company's profits, their jobs and, most important of all, their egos, on the line, the excitement is high and contagious. They are risking all, together. When it works out, the high level of business excitement translates very easily into sexual excitement. And so does catastrophic failure. When what they have been working on so intensely fails, it is a devastating blow to their egos—one that can be salvaged, perhaps, by turning to the other person who shared the work, the responsibility, and now, the failure. Together, they have given it their best. Now their mutual suffering can best be assuaged in mutual coupling. It is much more fun than suffering alone, particularly for sensation-seekers, who, according to Zuckerman, have a high sexual appetite to start with.

Two other opposite situations—cooperation and competition—seem to be equally strong aphrodisiacs. A man who is helpful, friendly, and cares about work the way you do can look like a Prince Charming. And a woman who is intelligent, concerned, always ready to help get the job done makes a man wonder how she looks with her glasses off.

The feeling aroused by competition between a man and a woman may be less loving but is also more exciting —something like a good tennis game between two skilled, equally matched opponents. The high-powered romances described by writers such as Michael Korda fit this description. The men and women involved play for high stakes, in and out of bed. All's fair in love and war, and for them, sex is an exciting combination of the two. Things can get nasty—think of Faye Dunaway in the film *Network*—but not always. The admiration and respect two high achievers feel for each other's talents can develop into a relationship that is rapturous and long-lasting, or at least highly satisfying while it lasts. Whether cooperation or competition sets it off, sexual attraction frequently starts with mutual admiration for each other's talent and style at work. The most exciting way to fall in love, in fact, may start with that most erogenous of all zones, the mind.

As we have seen, many opposite situations—success and failure, competition and cooperation, overwork and boredom—can produce equally strong sexual attractions. The explanation for this seeming paradox lies in a theory of human emotion first outlined by psychologist Stanley Schacter in 1964. Simply expressed, Schacter proposed that two factors must be present for us to feel emotion: we must be physiologically aroused—breathing hard, heart pounding, pulse racing; and we must have some reason for interpreting this arousal in emotional terms— as fear, as anger, as passion.

Since Schacter proposed his theory, it has been tested by him and by dozens of other researchers in experiments conducted in surroundings as commonplace as a laboratory or living room and as exotic as a slender bridge swaying high over a roaring river. The results have consistently supported Schacter's theory and extended it to show that the emotions we experience depend not so much on any particular physiological reaction or even what actually caused the reaction, but on what is going on around us—the social setting—when we feel the pounding heart and racing pulse.

Schacter was not talking specifically about feelings of love or sexual attraction, but his theory fits them beautifully. Our body's reactions—flushed face, quick heart beat, increased blood pressure—are much the same whether we are upset because someone has just yelled at us, elated because the boss has just praised our work, or angry because we just hit our thumb with a hammer. Whatever the cause, if there is a sympathetic, good-looking person around while we are aroused in this way, it is easy for us to translate the feeling into one of sexual interest. Or, as a psychologist friend so elegantly phrased it: "Physiological arousal affects the extent to which we experience an emotion when the opportunity for experiencing it comes along. In other words, when Mr. Right comes along, whether you get a charge out of him or let him pass by depends to a large extent upon whether you are, at this particular moment, hot to trot."

Working with psychologist Jerome Singer, Schacter

gave people a drug (ostensibly to test its effects on vision) that actually had effects similar to those of adrenaline: increased blood pressure and heartbeat, faster breathing, and a variety of other reactions like those that accompany human emotions. The researchers told some of the subjects what their reactions would be and didn't tell the rest. This meant that all the students would have the same physiological reactions; the difference would be how they would interpret them, which would depend on what they had been told to expect and what went on around them as they experienced the pounding heart, the rapid breathing, and so on.

After receiving the drug, the subjects were asked to go into various rooms and fill out a questionnaire. In some of the rooms, a man (actually a confederate of the experimenters) danced around, made paper airplanes out of the questionnaires, and generally acted humorously and mischievously. In other rooms, the confederate pretended to be angry, complained about the "stupid questions" they had to answer, and stormed out of the door. The experimenters watched all this through one-way mirrors.

Schacter and Singer found, as they expected, that students who had been given accurate information about the drug's effect did not imitate the confederate's actions or act particularly happy or angry. They knew why they were feeling what they did and had no need of an emotion to explain it. Most of the students who didn't know about the drug's effects followed the confederate's lead and seemed to share his happiness or anger.

In another experiment, Schacter manipulated just the physiological arousal and kept the emotion-arousing event the same. He gave some people adrenaline, some a tranquilizer, and the rest a placebo that had no physical effect. All of them then watched a slapstick comedy. The people who had received the adrenaline laughed the loudest and most often; those who had the placebo were in the middle. Schacter thus demonstrated that the amount of arousal (in this case, increased by adrenaline or decreased by a tranquilizer) affects the extent to which we experience an emotion when the opportunity to express it comes along. Everyone saw the same picture, but it seemed funnier to the people who were more aroused.

Physiological arousal, then, is necessary for us to feel emotion, but what the emotion will be depends on what clues we have to interpret the arousal. Psychologist J. W. Brehm told one group of men that they would receive three fairly strong electric shocks as part of an experiment they had volunteered for. Another group of men who had agreed to take part in the same experiment were not told about any shocks. All the men were then introduced to a young woman and later asked how they liked her. The men who expected to be shocked said they liked her more, on the average, than did the others. The first group apparently translated the anxiety they were feeling about the upcoming shocks into a somewhat different emotion when they met the young woman.

Stuart Valens found that even a bogus physiological reaction can increase liking. He let male college students listen to what was supposedly the sound of their own amplified heartbeats while they looked at photographs of ten seminude women. In fact, the heartbeat sound was controlled by the experimenter, who increased and decreased it at random. Later, when the men rated the ten photographs for attractiveness, most of them picked as best-looking the women they thought had made their heart beat faster.

The ease with which someone can interpret the physiological arousal produced by anxiety or fear as sexual arousal was further demonstrated by psychologists Donald Dutton and Arthur Aron in a series of experiments in British Columbia. They compared the reactions of young men crossing two bridges. The first, Capilano Canyon Bridge, was a 450-foot-long, 5-foot-wide span that tilts and wobbles over a 230-foot drop to shallow rapids and rocks below. The other bridge was a solid structure built just 10 feet above a shallow rivulet.

After each man crossed the bridge, an interviewer approached him, explaining that she was doing a study of how scenic attractions affected creativity. She asked the man to write a brief story based on the picture of a young woman covering her face with one hand and reaching out with the other. The interviewer then put her name and phone number on a piece of paper and invited the man to call if he wanted more information about the experiment.

Judges, unaware of who wrote which story, rated the stories for sexual imagery. The men interviewed by a woman after crossing the anxiety-producing suspension bridge included much more sexual imagery than those interviewed by the same woman after crossing the low, solid bridge. Moreover, of the eighteen men who accepted the female interviewer's name and phone number after crossing the suspension bridge, nine called her later; only two of the sixteen men on the solid bridge made the call.

Dutton and Aron specifically cited Schacter's theory in interpreting their findings. Men who crossed the suspension bridge were naturally anxious and fearful, but when an attractive woman came up to them, they eagerly interpreted the feelings as sexual arousal and responded to her request accordingly. After all, whatever the pangs of possibly unrequited love, they beat feeling scared.

Whatever it is that draws us together—exhilaration

or anxiety, overwork or boredom—we use it as a spring-board for further emotional experiences, including love. What psychologists have demonstrated in these experiments, and hundreds more, has been written about in fact and fiction for as long as we have written records. Consider the effect war has on people: the quick wartime romance, poignantly sweet in the movies of the nineteen-forties; the love among the ruins found in any bombed city; and even vicious raping that has occurred after battles everywhere from ancient Greece to Vietnam. All these are dramatic examples of what psychologists have found in their academic research, and of what, in a calmer way, we experience in our jobs.

One of the impediments to romance (or even understanding) between men and woman is the variety of ways they perceive and interpret each other's actions. Both men and women send out constant nonverbal signals and nearly as constantly misinterpret them. The trouble with body language—as the scientists who valiantly try to understand it admit—is its complexity. But there are some consistent differences in how men and women perceive the signals they give and receive.

The simple act of looking at someone, for example, is really not so simple. When one man stares at another for longer than ten seconds, he is thought of as being hostile or aggressive. The act is a continuation of that old teenage favorite, the stare-down, that sociobiologists relate back to our animal roots. The same length of eye contact between a man and a woman is interpreted, especially by the man, as a sexual come-on.

While neither sex looks very long at someone they find unattractive or uninteresting, studies show that women do look at faces more than men do, and they establish eye contact more often. Looking into someone's eyes is considered a friendly gesture by most women—not a particularly sexy one, and certainly not hostile.

Touching also means different things to men and women. Men touch in a clear-cut power pyramid, from the top down: older men touch younger men, men who have less important jobs, and men on the same level—often as a put-down or an attempt to assert their superiority. The man who is touched has a choice. He can accept it as a fatherly pat; a brotherly, we're-all-in-this-together gesture; or as a hostile act, depending on who does it and when. Men touch women as an expression of the same power motives—"You Jane, Me Tarzan"—as well as for the sexual pleasure it gives them.

When a woman touches a man, the interpretation is almost always sexual, on both their parts—unless they work in an office where touching is still in vogue. During the 1960s and early 1970s, when sensitivity training was the corporate rage, touching became an accepted, nonsexual (in theory) part of the business scene, at least in certain enlightened areas. How much of this still exists is debatable. It seems more like a phenomenon whose time has gone. In the 1980s, if someone touches you, think of it in the old, sex-related terms, and you are probably nearer the truth.

One of the interesting gender differences in touching was reported by Nancy Henley in her book *Body Politics*. It has to do not so much with *who* does the touching but *what* gets touched. Psychologist Tuan Nguyan asked men and women what it meant when someone of the opposite sex touched various parts of their bodies. Women said that patting or stroking their face, hands, arms, or back was an expression of friendliness or love. When the touching extended to more erotic parts of the body—breasts and buttocks—the women interpreted it as sexual rather than affectionate. Men made no such distinctions. A touch was a touch and meant both sex and affection.

Body language started as a legitimate academic discipline, graduated to a position of glamour in the media, and has now, we hope, retired gracefully to the limbo of the scientific journals. It does, however, reveal something about gender differences that often lead to misunderstanding. Women lean forward when talking more often than men—a sign of friendliness but not necessarily of sexual interest, as it is for men. Women are also more willing than men to tolerate physical closeness without reading it as a sign of hostility, whether the person coming close is a man or a woman. Men, in contrast, consider their space violated when another man stands too close. If a woman comes close, they like the violation, but interpret it differently, which can lead to trouble.

Psychologist Albert Mehrabian used "shoulder orientation" (how far individuals turn toward or away from someone they are seated next to) as an indication of how they felt about the other person. He found what you would expect: people usually turn away, unconsciously, from someone they don't like and toward someone they do. Donn Byrne, a leading sex researcher, also confirmed this through his research. The more men and women liked each other, the closer together they stood.

Robert Sommer found the same thing in research on what he dubbed our "space bubble"—the boundaries we establish around ourselves to feel comfortable. When this personal space is invaded, we—especially men—feel hostile and annoyed. If the invader is a loved one, we accept and even encourage the invasion.

These differences in how men and women interpret each other's words and actions matter little when sexual attraction is mutual. When this happens, both men and women look at each other more often, gaze deeply into each other's eyes, stand closer together, and lean toward each other—all without misinterpretation on either side. Psychologist Zick Rubin found that couples who score high on his loving scale—he also has a liking scale, but that is another matter—look at each other more frequently than do less loving couples; they also gaze directly into each other's eyes more often. The look of love is quite apparent.

People who are having an affair, a fling, or a full-fledged romance are drawn to each other in all these ways, many of them subconscious. When we can't seem to stay out of our lover's office, when we continually steal quick little glances at him or her, when our hands are drawn to each other's bodies—we are showing each other that a strong attraction exists. We are also, incidentally, showing the rest of the office that something is up this quarter besides the sales figures.

We have concentrated in this chapter on the general psychological and sociological forces that encourage sexual relationships in any office. There are other factors, which we will discuss more fully in Chapters 7 and 8, that arouse or discourage romantic feelings in particular offices. A boss's attitude and demeanor, for example: does he or she engage in sexual banter or dislike it? Does the company have a dress code, formal or otherwise, that discourages dresses, blouses, or skirts that might be considered provocative? Is there an "office bar" nearby at which people regularly meet for lunch or for drinks after work? Is there a company policy—again, expressed or just understood—against dating someone from the same office?

The next chapter deals with one of the most important factors in encouraging or discouraging office romance: how co-workers react to anything from mild flirting to a full-fledged affair. Keeping a romance quiet is almost impossible in the average office. People find out, and how they react plays a major role in determining the longevity of the relationship and the effect it has on the lovers' future with the company.

SIX

Office Romance: The Co-worker Connection

I don't care what they do, just so they don't do it in the street and scare the horses.

6

For Mrs. Patrick Campbell, a famous actress and wit of the early twentieth century, this bon mot was more than a witticism. It was her way of decrying the sexual gossip that abounded in the theater of her time, some of it directed at her. She could have said it more simply—"Why doesn't everybody mind their own business?"—but then we wouldn't still be quoting her remark today.

Most of us enjoy hearing and passing on the latest tidbit about who is sleeping with whom, be they actors, politicians, or anyone else. Magazines like *People* and *Us* and scandal sheets such as the *Star* and *National Enquirer* build their success on this appetite for gossip. And when we tire of celebrities, gossip about the peccadillos of the people we work with is a good substitute.

The fact is, gossip and rumor run rampant in all organizations. Studies by sociologists and psychologists confirm that most people in offices consider the grapevine a more reliable source of information than official memos, speeches, or briefings.

Sociologists Robert Rosnow and Gary Fine point out another interesting fact about gossip in their book *Rumor and Gossip: The Social Psychology of Hearsay*. Gossip thrives in times of uncertainty and anxiety, whether they are caused by natural catastrophes, such as earthquakes or floods, or less dramatic but still stressful developments within business organizations. When layoffs are announced or bosses are being hired and fired, the office becomes fertile territory for rumors of all types. People like to appear knowledgeable about what is going on around them, and spreading the latest rumor feeds this need. Since no one likes the feeling of uncertainty that comes with not knowing what is happening, people are especially eager to believe what they hear during times of crisis or change. When a rumor has the added tang of sex, it spreads like a Malibu Canyon fire during a Santa Ana wind.

These are the conditions that existed at the Bendix Corporation when the supposed Agee-Cunningham romance hit the headlines. It seems likely that the problems Agee was having with his fellow executives were as much responsible for the gossip as anything he and Cunningham did. In its cover story, "Upheaval at Bendix," *Fortune* Magazine reported that Cunningham's promotion followed the ousting of company president William P. Panny by Agee and the simultaneous resignation of Jerome Jacobson, the company's executive vice-president in charge of strategic planning—a resignation that left the job open for Cunningham. Even before this happened, many ordinary workers at Bendix were concerned about *their* jobs. A recent decision of Agee's had led to the possible transfer or dismissal of 250 employees at one plant that employed 600 people.

At Bendix, the business gossip that normally accompanies rapid change in any company was heightened by sniggering speculation about Agee and Cunningham. According to the *Fortune* article: "One story going around Detroit has it that a number of Bendix executives went to Panny complaining about the Cunningham-Agee relationship, and that Panny was planning to take the matter to the board. The next day, so the story goes, Agee fired him before he had a chance." Ex-president Panny refused to comment on the matter, *Fortune* said, and Agee denied any link between the Cunningham issue and the president's firing.

The only unusual features of the flap at Bendix were the high level of the people involved and the national publicity it received. Employees love to gossip about bosses, whatever their rank. The fact that the boss in this case was the head of one of the country's major companies, and that his supposed inamorata was a blond, attractive whiz kid, simply spiced things up a bit. We usually make do with blander corporate fare.

The ability to stand up to co-worker gossip is a constant test for office relationships. Even in these supposedly liberated times, many people automatically look down on any sort of sexual relationship short of love and marriage and try to destroy it, with gossip a prime weapon. Others don't care about the sex; their objections are purely economic. Either they think the lovers are sloughing off on their jobs, leaving more work for them, or they fear that one of the lovers will get favored treatment from the other—in terms of better job assignments, promotions, or salary boosts. Whatever the motive, the gossip it engenders can go a long way toward breaking up a relationship.

The pervasiveness of office gossip is one reason most couples try to keep their liaisons secret from co-workers. A love affair offers enough problems on its own without the whole office keeping score, cheering, or booing from the sidelines. Fellow workers can throw cold water on a sizzling affair faster than a city kid can open a fire hydrant in August. An advertising manager explains how he learned this the hard way: "I've kept my love life and office life completely separate since what happened two years ago. I started going out with one of our new sales promotion people, and for a while everything was fine. I even thought it might develop into something permanent. And as long as Joan and I saw each other only after work, there were no problems. But as soon as we went public—I would stop by her desk, she would come to my office, we started going to lunch together—the hassles began. At first the questions and remarks were friendly, if a bit prying. 'How is Joan these days? I understand you're seeing a lot of her.'

"Then the remarks started to have an edge, particularly after Joan was given a chance to handle one of our new product lines. Hell, it wasn't even my idea. The sales supervisor said she'd been doing good work and he wanted to see what she could do with something new, starting from scratch. But a lot of people seemed to think I set the whole thing up. Joan said she was getting the cold shoulder from people in her department, too.

"I guess we started blaming each other, subconsciously at least, for the problems we were having. Blame and romance are a bad combination, and we finally stopped seeing each other. It just became too much for both of us. When Joan got a chance for a job in Chicago, she jumped at it. I haven't seen her since. She called once when she was in town a few months ago. We talked about having lunch but things just didn't work out. I guess neither of us really tried too hard to make them work."

Other people usually have this negative effect on office romances, but occasionally they act as catalysts. They see who is eyeing whom, and then, through hints and innuendos, push the two hesitant oglers into each other's arms. One attractive woman described how this happened to her. At first, she simply enjoyed talking to a man at work because he made her feel good. "We both

just seemed brighter and sharper when we were together,'' she explained. This mutual attraction was duly
noted by the rest of the staff, until one day at lunch a
friend asked if she was having an affair with the man. ''I
was truly astounded,'' she told us. ''The thought had
never entered my mind—but it did then. I'm not sure what
changed, but I began to see him in a different and definitely sexier light. I didn't consciously start to give off
signals, but within a few weeks of that lunch, Mark and I
were having an affair.''

In this case, the woman didn't care about office gossip. It wasn't any worse once the affair actually started
than it had been before. She felt, to paraphrase the old
adage, that she might as well have the game as the name.

Fellow workers can be more than the kindling that
starts a romance. Their gossip can also be the bellows
that keeps the flame going. For some men and women,
knowing that people are talking about them is an important
part of the excitement. They need to be noticed, to be the
Don Juan or femme fatale of the office. If their fling isn't
noticed—and, better still, disapproved of—the excitement
dies down quickly. Couples who feel this way are the ones
who take more and more chances of being discovered in
compromising situations in the office itself. The thrill of
being discovered in the act is as exciting as the act itself.

If a romance doesn't seem to hurt anybody or affect
anyone's job directly, it can actually improve office morale
by sparking other people's imaginations and giving them
something juicy to talk about. We are all voyeurs to some
extent, so the heavy breathing and disheveled appearance
of a man and a woman after they have been grappling in
the stockroom or the speculation of who's seeing whom
after hours adds zest to the coffee break gossip. Whether
or not management officially frowns on such gossip, to

most of us it is just another office perk, and not the least important. We know of one boss who, before his staff left for an annual sales meeting, announced that "no bed checking" was his rule. Who went with whom, and what they did, was nobody's business but their own. Despite these brave words, gossip about who was never in her own room, and who was making it with whom was discussed and documented in great detail—certainly more fully than business matters were covered in the formal convention reports produced by the staff.

Sexual relationships develop in offices for a variety of reasons, and in many different ways, as we've discussed. But however a relationship develops, other people soon realize something is going on. In his study of office affairs, psychologist Robert Quinn of the State University of New York at Albany, asked several hundred people what usually tipped them off. The three most popular clues, he reports, were that the lovers were seen together away from work, spent an unusual amount of time talking at work, or took long lunch hours. They usually tried to keep the affair secret, especially at the beginning, but many times one or the other really wanted others to know and made sure they did. In Quinn's words: "If an individual's motive in establishing a romantic relationship partially stems from the need to demonstrate his or her social worth, the person also needs to let others know of the accomplishment."

Some lovers did this blatantly—making sure people saw them together in a popular dining spot, being caught hugging, kissing, or worse in the stock room—and some were positively Machiavellian. One woman told Quinn how an executive asked a woman in his department to pick out a nice dress of a certain size and type. "Thinking that the dress was a surprise for his wife, the woman complied. Two days later, another member of the staff showed up wearing the dress.''

Whatever a romance does for the two people directly involved, it usually causes problems for the people around them. Based on Quinn's study, office romance has a positive effect only about 10 percent of the time. He cites one case in which a male supervisor, known for years as sloppy and disorganized, straightened out both personally and organizationally when he became involved with a woman in his office. His ties began to match his suit, his memos became more coherent, and he started getting to work on time.

In another incident, the female head of a personnel department had developed a reputation as being hard to get along with. She was particularly disliked by the accounting department, until romance bloomed between her and a man in accounting. From then on, relations became less tense between the departments.

Unfortunately, such positive results were the exception in Quinn's study. Usually people complained that the lovers either were too preoccupied with each other to do their work properly—they missed meetings, arrived late and left early, made costly errors—or that they showed favoritism to their beloved. In the case of the men, who usually held the better jobs, this favoritism showed up in unjustified promotions, easier assignments, or more power for their lovers. The women, reciprocating, covered up the men's mistakes, flaunted their new power, or, in one case Quinn mentions, ''became an extended set of eyes and ears for the boss by reporting comments and actions that normally would not have reached him.''

Naturally enough, such actions made other people in the department unhappy. The most common response was going to the lover they knew best to point out how the af-

fair was creating problems for everyone else. When this
didn't work, as it usually didn't, the aggrieved co-workers
complained to their immediate supervisor or took more
direct action—sabotaging the person's work or ostraciz-
ing him or her socially. In one case, Quinn said, "members of a steno pool stole files and hid parts of projects
that one romantically involved secretary was working on.
In another case, subordinates leaked damaging information about the work of their boss to a regulatory agency."

Eventually, through complaints from the staff or
their own observations, management usually heard about
the romance and the problems it caused. The most common response, Quinn found, was to ignore the situation.
Some managers felt the situation was just too personal
for them to get involved in. They were embarrassed and
hoped it would go away. Others felt they were in a no-win
situation, whatever they did. As one man put it, "If the
guy denies that a relationship exists, what do you say
then?" Quinn found that about one-quarter of the time a
manager called one or both of the lovers in, discussed the
matter openly, and tried to come up with a solution. Ten
percent of the time a manager took punitive action. He
reprimanded, transferred, warned, or fired someone; and
it was usually the woman who was fired. In the cases
Quinn heard about, women were dismissed twice as often
as men.

Quinn reported that most of the people he interviewed were more than willing to talk about office romance—a fact we quickly discovered for ourselves. All we
had to do was mention what our book was about, and we
heard: "Let me tell you what's been going on in our office." The details varied, of course, but certain patterns
kept cropping up in how people learn of an affair, why
they approved or didn't, and what they did about it.

For example, several women in the sales department of a large international corporation told us about a young man in the accounting department who was sleeping with the receptionist. How did they know? Well, "He is constantly hanging around her desk. . . . She always brings him his messages personally, instead of just leaving a note or calling him on the phone, the way she does for everyone else. . . . They've started leaving for lunch at the same time. . . ."

No one objected to the liaison on moral grounds, or so they said. And there was no indication that anyone was being harassed or exploited in the relationship. Yet we sensed a general air of disapproval, a snicker in some voices when they talked about the receptionist, a "what would you expect of her" attitude from others. It became obvious, as we listened, that the disapproval was aimed almost exclusively at the receptionist rather than her lover.

While this particular office was anything but a hotbed of feminism, the women justified their disapproval by insisting that the receptionist was letting them down—that her involvement undermined their chances to appear as professional and as competent as the men in the office. "It's tacky," one woman said firmly.

It was revealing—and consistent with what we saw in other offices—that this disapproval concerned someone who held a lower-level job. When we asked the same women about another rumored affair between two highly placed officers of the company, their reactions were much different. Most of them felt it was all very glamorous and exciting—trips to Bermuda, champagne, and caviar. Not the least bit tacky. The romance they disapproved of was more like Coney Island, beer, and pretzels.

There was no indication that either affair was disrupting work in the office, that either party was using it to advance his or her career or obtain special favors, except sexual ones. Whether jealousy of the receptionist, strengthened by a bit of snobbery, entered into the appraisals, or if the women really were concerned about how the affair would reflect on them, we can't be sure. But their concern is a legitimate one in today's business world. One of the favorite arguments used in the past to keep women out of higher-ranking jobs was the supposed fear that throwing men and women together would result in orgies, bacchanals, or just plain fooling around. The resulting taboos against traveling together, late nights, or close quarters of any kind have all been used to keep women in their place: the bottom of the corporate ladder. It is significant that while a man traveling with his secretary might be suspected of hanky-panky, the arrangement was accepted in most companies for many years. She was, after all, just a secretary. A woman who traveled with a man as an equal was (and often still is) perceived as a threat—a wanton, a threat to hearth and home. Even worse, she might just end up on top.

Jealousy is a particularly strong element in office gossip when the boss is involved. Any woman who occupies what others think is an undue amount of a boss's time can expect innuendos, hostility, and vindictiveness from her co-workers, regardless of whether there is any reason to suspect an affair. (We have used the male boss/female subordinate relationship as an example because it is by far the most common one, but the gossip and unhappy reactions are at least as strong when a woman is the boss.)

A West Coast magazine editor related what happened when he moved up to replace a woman as assistant managing editor. "After a month or so on the job," Frank told us, "I thought I understood it pretty well, but there was one thing that still puzzled me. I couldn't figure out what I was supposed to talk to the managing editor about that would take two hours a day." That was about how long Helen, his predecessor, averaged in her boss's office. When we asked Frank if he felt something had been going on, he laughed and said, "If you mean an affair, no. But I'm sure she was interested. I just don't think he was."

Frank's reaction seemed good-natured, but as we talked to others on the magazine, we found a great deal of animosity toward Helen and huge sighs of relief that she had finally left. Some of this feeling stemmed from her personality. She had a sharp tongue and no compunction about using it to put down others at meetings. But there was jealousy too, much of it centering on the inordinate amount of time—or so it seemed to her co-workers—that she spent in the managing editor's office. After she left, the matter was turned into a running joke. Whenever anyone spent more than a few minutes with the managing editor, the offender was accused of "pulling a Helen." Professional jealousy, an element in this case, often results from the stress of competition, particularly when an assertive woman seems to be winning out. The kidding remarks by Frank and the rest of the staff may well have masked underlying feelings of insecurity and stress.

The size of an office staff, the business or industry involved, the positions the lovers hold in the organization —all of these influence the tone of the gossip aroused by the liaison. But they don't have much effect on what people finally do when they feel a romance is directly affecting or disrupting their jobs.

In a small office—fewer than ten people, say—reactions are usually quicker and stronger than when there are more people involved. And when the boss is one of the lovers, matters are especially sticky, as a woman named Karen told us. Fresh out of college, she took a job in the four-person Washington, D.C., office of a small nonprofit association. Within the first few weeks, the secretary told Karen she was having an affair with the executive director and, a bit later, confided that she knew he was also carrying on with the assistant director.

"I was amazed," Karen admits. "None of them were particularly attractive. He was in his forties, married, had three kids, and was sort of a wimp. Both of the women were married, too. It was really sick. He kept a rolled-up mattress in his file cabinet, ready to spread out for fun and games.

"At first I couldn't believe what I heard and saw. I remember going to see my parents and asking them if it was normal for this guy to be having affairs with both women in the office. There was silence for a few seconds, and then my mother asked, 'Sam, has anything like that ever happened where you worked?' My dad smiled, and, ever the diplomat, explained that, 'I've always worked in places with a hundred or more people. If any man was having affairs with two-thirds of the women there, he would've been dead.'

"Obviously, he wasn't too surprised, and certainly not appalled by what I'd told them. So I thought, 'Well, that's just the way things are in the business world.' I still didn't like the situation, but since I had accepted the job, I thought I should stay at least a year. I thought that's what good girls did. But things kept getting weirder and weirder.

"It was just too small an office and I got too involved

in their crazy private lives. It was like a soap opera. You started to get hooked on the story line, and then it's too late to say you don't want to hear any more. My only way out was to quit."

This is an extreme case, admittedly, but it shows how particularly sensitive small offices are to sexual upset. No matter how careful the people are, a quick turnover of personnel is usually one costly offspring of small office philandering. In larger offices, the effects of sexual dalliance normally take longer to be felt, but eventually what is going on becomes grist for the rumor mill. In these cases, staff members who feel morally or otherwise upset by what is happening have higher authorities to complain to. When they do, as we mentioned earlier, any action management takes to end the affair—reprimand, transfer, or firing—usually falls most heavily on the woman involved. This is less costly and troublesome for the company, since she almost always has the lower-ranking job.

Occasionally, a boss's philandering opens a Pandora's box for him as well. This happened to the second-in-command in the advertising department of a large consumer products corporation. He had suffered a series of personal problems, including the death of his wife. As a result, his staff tolerated and covered for his frequent erratic behavior. When he started dating a young woman who had recently been hired as a typist, most people were happy for him. But when he tried to promote her to the job of office manager—a position that was highly sensitive since the office manager supervised all work and expense accounts—the resentment that had been slowly building toward him during the previous months exploded. No one wanted their problems to become pillow talk for the boss. Men and women alike protested the promotion, quietly at first and then with increasing fervor. Long-hidden stories of the man's mistakes, pill-popping, and sometimes contradictory orders were revealed. Within two months of the time he tried to promote his girlfriend, he was fired.

Whether the staff would have continued to care and cover for him if his romance hadn't interfered with business, no one will ever know. Perhaps they were just waiting for an excuse to discuss his deficiencies with his boss and simply used the affair as a *cause célèbre*. But use it they did, and, in this case, the boss got the ax.

An affair that results in someone receiving special treatment is a prime cause of discontent. When bosses get the objects of their affection promotions, raises, more interesting work, or more perks such as trips out of town, you can bet the gossip level will raise and trouble will start. The same reaction occurs when an affair starts to affect the quality or quantity of work being turned out by the people involved, particularly if this means more work for others or jeopardizes an ongoing project.

When one or both of the people involved is married, or if it seems clear that one is using the other, co-workers often feel a moral duty to cool things down. This is particularly true when people have close social relationships outside the office. One case we heard about involved a new, small (thirty-person) solar energy company. Since its people had been brought in from all over the country and most were strangers to the area, they developed into a close-knit group at work and play. Most of them had families who were also included in the formal and informal gatherings that took place in the office as well as at private homes. This family feeling and participation was encouraged by the owners of the firm, who believed it was good for morale.

For more than a year, most of the people there felt they had the best of both worlds—work and play—in an ideal setting. But then the serpent entered the Garden of Eden in the form of an affair between the recently hired daughter of the head of accounting and a married salesman. The relationship had a much more devastating effect on the workings of this company than it would have had in a less close-knit group. To some, the relationship seemed almost incestuous. The situation embarrassed the young woman's father and disrupted the easy give and take among the staff and their families, particularly the relationship with the salesman and his wife.

The social side of the company began to fall apart as people took sides. A few felt the whole thing was none of their business, while others were appalled, furious, or just plain nonplussed by the situation. They felt involved but didn't know what to do about it. The owner did not interfere directly, but he did cancel some of the business functions that had always doubled as family social affairs. Matters finally ended quietly when the young woman moved to another town and another job. The salesman also left the company a few months later.

In talking with several members of the staff about what had happened, it became clear that the familylike atmosphere had changed considerably. "We seem to be growing apart," one man told us. "It probably would have happened anyway, as we got to know more people in town. And maybe that's better, maybe your job shouldn't become too much of your social life.

"But at the beginning it seemed so great. To be working and almost living with a group of people who shared the same ideas and interests, to see our kids together. It wasn't a commune, but we were about as close as any group of people that aren't blood-related can be. I'm just sorry the change started because of some kid with hot pants and an aging Romeo. I wish it had happened naturally instead of bitterly. The job is still OK, the company is fine, and we still have friends there. We're just not living in each others pockets any more."

People who work together in offices are, in a sense, living in each other's pockets, at least for eight hours a day. There is a coziness to this, with the right people. But it is a delicate balance, easily disturbed by strong feelings such as love, lust, and jealousy. The old-fashioned company rules about no dating among employees were unfair, unenforceable, and maybe even unconstitutional, if you had a good lawyer. But they recognized a simple truth. All the world does *not* love a lover, particularly if he or she is working at the next desk or just down the hall and seems to be getting favored treatment for being a lover.

Handling situations like these that cause resentment, jealousy, and gossip is a challenge for any company, no matter how liberated or well-intentioned. Office relationships can be very intense, creating rivalries and feelings nearly as strong as those between siblings, or between parents and children. In a very real sense, the office *is* a family, one held together by emotional ties as well as economic needs. In the next chapter we will examine the nature and quality of these ties—what they are and how they help or hinder the development of sexual relationships in the office.

SEVEN

THE OFFICE FAMILY

7

THE COMPANY HAS ALWAYS BEEN a part-time family for many people and a full-time family for a few. As nearly half our marriages break up in divorce, and as people move from job to job and town to town as a normal part of their working lives, the idea of corporation as family becomes more compelling. If Eloise or Sam has moved out, and you don't really know the people next door—in fact, they aren't the same people who lived there last month—it is comforting to find a substitute sibling or parent in the office.

This isn't necessarily bad. We spend so much time at work that it is only normal to feel some special relationship with the people there. This special feeling can be pleasant and even useful, unless it is carried to the point where "family feelings" become more important than work. Projecting all your normal need for affection and caring on fellow workers is asking for trouble, however. The family roles we expect others to play, and that they expect of us, become so compelling that they deprive us of the opportunity to grow and succeed on the job as ourselves, without being shackled by the expectations of others. As Massachusetts management consultant Jeanne Bosson Driscoll pointed out in a *Management Review* article: "Men and women often view persons of the opposite sex in roles that provide them with the greatest comfort and treat others, therefore, as their children, parents, or spouses. This is easier and less threatening than learning to work together as equals."

But just as the American family at home has undergone enormous changes in the past decade or two, so has the corporate family. And just as changes in the home family structure and in the relationships among the members of these families have forced them to see each other in new ways, so the office family must adjust and accept a new structure and new roles.

The most significant recent change in the office family is the growing role played by women. There are more women working, of course, but their impact involves much more than sheer numbers. Women are doing many jobs they seldom did before, working on a more equal footing with men in these jobs and others, and moving up the executive ladder to more responsible positions.

How fully they are accepted by their peers, their subordinates, and their superiors varies greatly from company to company. Just as each family has its own personality, so does each office. That's why the first things most of us do in a new job are size up the social atmosphere and try to figure out the relationships among the people who work there. Some offices are formal; there are firm pecking orders and rules to be followed in social settings as well as in business matters. At these offices, you don't find a shirt-sleeved boss whose door is always open, nor people chatting on a first-name basis with the boss. Other offices go to the opposite extreme, with an atmosphere so relaxed and consciously egalitarian that it takes a while to figure out who is in charge of what. The atmosphere, whatever it is, normally comes from the top. The basic tone is set by management, although supervisors or managers can modify it through their personal styles.

Lower-level employees have less effect, but how they accept or react to the tone they find influences the overall atmosphere. It usually doesn't take long for a new man or woman to realize how to dress, talk, and socialize to get along in a new job. This kind of acclimatization is just as important in the relationship between men and women as it is on the business side. Both sexes take note of how much socialization goes on, and how it is transacted. Is sexual banter frowned upon, tolerated, or encouraged? Do people have lunch together, or go out for drinks, on the basis of job classification, age, sex, or catch-as-catch-can? Reading these signs correctly and conforming to them play a big part in determining how well someone does in a company. To play the office game well, you must know the rules—the unwritten social and status code as well as the formal procedures and regulations.

For all the psychological reasons discussed in Chapter 5, almost any office is a potential hotbed of sexuality. How far this potential becomes reality depends on several factors: the image a particular business or industry projects, the attitudes top management has toward women, and the managerial style and approach of individual bosses. Let's look at these factors individually and see how they interact to heat up or cool down the sexual temperature—and the degree of sexual equality—in a particular office.

Some businesses—computer companies, banks, insurance companies, and other financial institutions are good examples—present an image of straightlaced conservatism. The offices are businesslike and formal, as is the dress and attitudes of the people who work there. Sex just doesn't seem to fit. This is certainly not always the case, for reasons we'll discuss later, but the image is strong. Other fields of business, notably glamour industries such as advertising, publishing, fashion, and television, have the reputation for offering a much freer, more liberal atmosphere in which sexual activity is condoned and perhaps actively encouraged. Much of this is strictly hype, at which people in these fields are professionally adept. The fact is, if the amount of sex play you hear about really did go on in the communications fields, little would ever be printed, produced, or aired. The people involved wouldn't have enough time or energy left to do their jobs.

But, even allowing for exaggeration, communications companies are certainly more liberal in their sexual attitudes than IBM, IT&T, or your local savings and loan institution. Much of this freedom simply comes with the territory. Ad agencies, fashion houses, and the like all use sex to sell their products, while magazines and newspapers are just as savvy about the ability of a good sex scandal to entice subscribers and newsstand sales. With so much sex around them in their jobs, a little personal experimentation is only natural.

The supposed connection between creativity and sexual gymnastics is another factor used to explain the lenient attitudes media companies take toward the actions of their "creative people." Whether there is any connection is a moot point. But since anything that you believe enhances your creativity or sexual prowess probably does just that, the belief in a tie-in between sex and creativity may simply be another self-fulfilling prophecy.

There is also a certain amount of pride involved in stories about what goes in communications companies. Swapping bigger and better tales of sexual comings and goings in your office can become as much of a contest between magazines or ad agencies as their competition in summer softball leagues. Each side wants to claim the title as the hottest bed-hopping shop in town. One former *Time* editor, hearing about our book, said pridefully, "Hell, Time, Inc., invented sex in the office."

In theater, television, and movies, the fabled casting couch may have seen more action in the old days, but sex is still an important part of the act. The old publicity game that torrid love scenes between the stars are just as hot off the stage or screen is as popular as ever.

Work conditions at magazines and other media companies encourage flings rather than longer-term relationships. You work closely with someone for a week or a month, and then you move on to the next assignment, usually with someone else. The job often involves travel, odd working hours, and on occasion, exotic settings—all conditions likely to encourage togetherness. To many, the ensuing sex is a natural part of the recreational repast. Since it is expected, the men and the women involved are less discrete than in most other lines of work, and gossip is likely to be less critical, if more graphic.

Anyone who works in these fields will obviously have more opportunities for sexual liaisons without fear of disapproval from bosses or peers. This freedom can have its bad side too. If a relationship sours and one of the people involved feels he or she has been hurt and used by the other, the injured party isn't likely to get, or expect, much sympathy from other people in the office. Their attitude will probably be that it comes with the territory. If you want to play the game, in these fields, you should be smart and sophisticated enough to shrug off one affair and move on to the next.

While different fields do have different sexual auras, the vibrations within any particular company, regardless of the field, are influenced strongly by the attitudes of top management. How men in an office think about and act toward the women they work with can often be traced to top-level policies and examples. If a company's upper-level executives seem to respect women for the work they do and reward them with raises, promotions, and new opportunities, other men are likely to follow the lead and treat their female co-workers with similar respect. But if a company downgrades women's contributions and seems to regard them as good for only two things—handling routine work and looking decorative—this negative attitude is reflected in contacts between men and women in its offices.

What happened to one young woman executive at a national convention she attended for a tobacco company is a case in point. At a party given by her employer for salesmen and customers, her boss introduced her to a man she had heard of and admired for his work with community projects. He immediately propositioned her in a way that was as vulgar as it was straightforward. Her boss laughed, said, ''I'm sure you can handle this yourself,'' and walked away. Later, after she had painfully extricated herself from the situation, she found that her company was well known for hiring prostitutes to keep customers happy at conventions. Obviously, the man had presumed she was one of them.

When we first heard this story, we assumed it was an isolated case. We were wrong. Several other women told us of being propositioned because the company or man they worked for had a reputation for making women available for customers or other friends of the firm.

The idea that sex sells is used a bit more subtly by companies who hire a model, put her in a bikini, and have her point out—as provocatively as possible—the advantages of, say, a new hydraulic system. The fact she may have no idea what the system is or does doesn't matter. In the same way, women employees picked to promote products at meetings and conventions are often selected for their good looks rather than their knowledge of the product—the criteria used for picking their male compatriots.

To give just one example from the half dozen we heard, the sales executives of a housewares company held a meeting to decide who should staff the company booth at their trade association's national convention. One unanimous choice, among the men, seemed to be "sexy Mona," who all agreed was "a good party girl." When several of the women at the meeting objected to the comments, the men accused them of having something against Mona. They were only kidding, the men explained, when they talked about her as a good party girl. She was really well qualified for the job, by her sales record, her product knowledge, and the part she had played in developing sales promotion material for the convention. Her other, less cerebral qualities were just "icing on the cake." When the women continued to protest, the sales director told them to drop the matter, stop causing trouble, and get back to the business at hand. The most surprising part about this story, according to the woman we heard it from, was that the company's top officers prided themselves on the firm's liberal attitudes toward women.

The anecdote illustrates a situation we found in many companies. Word from the top called for equality of opportunity and the elimination of sexism in all areas of company life. At the department level, however, managers continued to hire women chiefly for their looks rather than their business savvy or potential, and there were no women in a managerial or supervisory role in the department. Sending memos decrying harassment or sponsoring occasional meetings to change sexist attitudes doesn't do much good without strong, consistent follow-up from the top to see that the methods and practices of lower-level executives implement the sweet-sounding policies proclaimed in memos and meetings.

Another unfortunate truth, we discovered, is that positive attitudes from top management don't have nearly as powerful an effect as negative ones. In cases where high-level executives project a sexist image, women become fair game throughout the company. Without strong backing from the top, it's very hard for anyone on a lower level to change the sexist status quo without a series of suits and threats of suits charging harassment and discrimination. Even then, unless there is an honest change of heart among the corporate echelon, any positive action that occurs will be grudging and tentative, reflecting the attitude that "the government has stuck its nose in our business and we have to comply." With this feeling in the air, compliance is likely to be minimal, and the situation will probably not improve very much.

Even when executives at all levels are honestly trying to change their company's ways and encourage acceptance of women as peers, they face a hidden problem: an almost reflex desire by many men to protect other men from what they see as feminist assaults. In one case reported by a management consultant, a production line supervisor who for years had been sexually harassing his female workers and downgrading their work was finally removed from his job. But since no one on the staff was told specifically why he was dismissed, management missed a perfect opportunity to stress its disapproval of such conduct, and to use the man's firing as proof that the company meant what it said about sexual harassment. When the management consultant asked about this, he was told that no one wanted to hurt the man's reputation or injure his chances for getting another job. The fact that his reputation among the women workers, at least, was already as bad as it could be did not seem to matter.

A situation like this is embarrassing for everyone. It is particularly hard for the personnel officer or other management person who handled the case to be completely honest about what has happened. But it should be just as important to consider the feelings of all employees, not just the man who broke the rules. In this case, unfortunately, management chose to close ranks and sweep the case under the rug; they protected one man but missed an opportunity to give hope and encouragement to many women.

Another factor that heats or cools an office's sexual temperature is the managerial style and attitude of individual bosses. Some managers, for example, actively encourage a sexual atmosphere in the name of promoting happiness and harmony among the members of their staff. In his book *The Gamesman,* Michael Maccoby describes Wakefield, a "creative gamesman," who has an "ability to create an environment where others work better." According to Wakefield's secretary, one way he accomplished this was to "throw a beer bust every six weeks or so. He had us (the secretaries) roam through the crowd and make sure people didn't discuss business."

Maccoby notes that "there was a gamey, sexy atmosphere to the office. The men were encouraged to trade sexy, spicy repartee with the girls, who played a function that sometimes seemed a combination of Playboy bunny and housemother."

Maccoby also quotes the secretary as saying, "When I first came here, I found that if I smiled freely, it would make the day for some of the guys. When I first started wearing hot pants to work, Wakefield kidded me about it. But then he told me to wear a certain outfit if he was going to have a bad day. I like being a girl here. I've never felt that being a girl has hurt me. They don't treat me as dumb or anything. They really appreciate it.''

Maccoby's ''creative gamesman'' is a prime example of how a boss can set an office tone. If he (or, rarely, she) creates a party atmosphere and encourages sexual banter, there will be a much more sexual tone than there is in an office run by someone who feels an aura of sexuality is not the right one for a business office.

Wakefield constantly flattered the secretaries and told them how much power they had in influencing the atmosphere of the office. Maccoby did not go into the consequences of the deliberately sexy mood created by Wakefield. He doesn't say whether affairs were common or what happened if one of the women decided she didn't want to be a Playboy bunny for the office. According to Maccoby, Wakefield just wanted to make people feel good and therefore work better; but apparently he never realized that the means he used created an image of women as sexual objects rather than workers. This set up a no-win situation for any woman who resented the atmosphere. She either had to leave her job, or, if she stayed with it, be unhappy knowing that she was considered a spoilsport or ''libber'' by the rest of the staff.

Wakefield was asking women to play the temptress, a role that many find flattering and attractive. After all, it gives the outward appearance, at least, of power. But accepting and playing the temptress role reinforces the stereotypes most women are fighting to overcome in the business world.

Freud said that men place women in one of two categories: madonna or whore. This is an oversimplification of how most men feel about women and of what Freud meant, but it is a convenient way of dividing the labels many men unconsciously give the women they work with: the mother, the tomboy, the kid sister, the baby girl, the iron maiden, the temptress, the wife. These categories, and our thumbnail descriptions of them, are variations on roles described by sociologist Rosabeth Kanter in her book *Men and Women of the Corporation* (1977). She was writing specifically about token women in the office, but we found that many women we talked to, token or not, are being cast in similar roles today. Kanter did not deal specifically with sexual relationships in the office, but she was aware that they did exist and strongly affected the people and the corporation.

The mother, often older than most of the other women in an office, is always ready to listen to problems; she is invariably sympathetic, consistently supportive, and puts the needs of others before her own. In simple terms, she babies the men on the staff, at least those who will permit it. One of the women we interviewed told us about a man who actually talked baby talk to his office mother.

The tomboy is one of the boys, a role she may fill in a number of ways. She may be a sports buff; she may win her spurs by drinking the boys under the table; she may tolerate the dirty stories or tell a few of her own. Whatever her specialty, she sees herself as different from the other women and would rather associate with the men, on or off the job.

The kid sister is similar to the tomboy in some ways, but she projects a softer, more traditionally feminine image. She is considered cute and is expected to be cheerful and helpful at all times—a mother in training. In return, the men protect her, and most of the women in the office like her better than they do the tomboy.

The baby girl is equally protected but occupies a lower rung on the office prestige ladder. She may become the kid sister if the incumbent outgrows the part or leaves to take another job. The baby girl is another role that usually can't last long, unless the woman is exceptionally pretty and demure. Usually all the men see her as vulnerable and vie to protect her, but she often ends up with one big daddy in particular, one special pair of broad shoulders to lean on. She is likely to drive the other women in the office slightly mad. It is hard to compete with someone cuddled up on a man's lap, literally or figuratively.

The iron maiden is made of different stuff entirely. She sometimes plays the stern teacher and can be counted on to keep other employees toeing the corporate line. More women have won the iron maiden label in recent years as they strive to keep their work and social lives completely separate, insisting that they are in the office to do a good job, and get ahead, with no social distractions. Iron maidens sometimes do well in organizations, but they are limited by the fact that the chief emotions they inspire are fear or ridicule rather than the respect that is important to reaching a high-level job.

All the roles we've talked about so far fall under the madonna category. Even the tomboy is usually not thought of in any serious sexual way, since it is hard to be considered one of the boys and one of the girls at the same time. This leaves the whore role to the *temptress* or *femme fatale*. Actually, this multifaceted role can be played in a number of different ways (and often is, by several women in the same office): the office flirt, the office tart, or any of the roles between. Physical contact may occur somewhere along the line, but the temptress's main function within the office is as a fantasy object, someone to keep the men happy and hoping by being consistently sexy and attractive. At best, she even acts as a safety valve, protecting the other women's roles by filling her part and thereby keeping the office play running smoothly.

The final category is the *office wife*. She is usually a secretary—often called a personal secretary—to someone fairly high up in management. The term is peculiarly apt because the woman often handles as many personal matters as business ones. She keeps things neat and organized, makes coffee—unless she is an executive secretary; then she usually delegates the brewing to someone else—balances her boss's checkbook, buys gifts for his wife, and generally oversees his personal and business comfort. She often feels a very real emotional commitment to him; and he, in turn, relies on her much as he does his real wife—often even more, since he is paying his secretary.

The secretary's reward, in many cases, is that as he moves up the corporate ladder, she rises with him. This is highly gratifying to many women, who take vicarious pleasure in their boss's success and also feel that riding his coattails offers their best route to higher salary and greater status. Such wholehearted commitment to someone else's career makes it hard to leave a boss even when there is a chance to move on to a higher-level job. In her book, Kanter capsulized the situation: a secretary who left her longtime boss to accept a promotion told Kanter she "felt as if she had gotten a divorce" from him.

Becoming this deeply involved usually has one of two results: bad or worse. At best, it stifles individuality and ambition and eliminates any real chance for personal advancement; second best is the best you can hope for. At worst, the "office husband" is transferred, quits to take another job, is fired, or otherwise becomes divorced from his faithful companion, leaving her with custody of the desk and little else.

All this role-playing often works pretty well, in the short run, as long as everybody feels comfortable in their roles. And they often do, because their role at the office is similar to the one they play at home. The office mother may be a biological mother as well, or at least an elder sister. The kid sister, the baby girl, and the tomboy often have brothers or fathers who treat them the same way they are treated in the office. The iron maiden may come from an authoritarian family where father was law. And the temptress was the school vamp—a woman who has always been aware of her effect on men and has been willing to trade on it. Some women accept these roles because they feel comfortable in them. For others, it is simply easier to go along with the crowd and be accepted for that quality than it is to fight to change the image.

So the office play goes on. As long as all the actors know their lines and stay in character, it works. But when someone tries to shed her role, or a man makes a serious pass at the kid sister, the baby girl, or, God forbid, the mother, all hell breaks loose. Incest has been committed, figuratively at least, and someone must be punished. (That someone is still usually the woman or women involved, who ''should have known better.'')

Playing a familiar role is comfortable. Ask any actor in a long-running Broadway play. But it is also ultimately boring and limiting. People can't express themselves fully—in their personal lives or their careers—if they are limited by traditional and stagnant definitions of what they are and can be. Because traditional values and ideas die hard, women are still being looked upon in ways that smack of their old, in some ways more comfortable, roles as symbols, family members, and servants. These outmoded attitudes create problems for everyone—for the women who are restricted by them; for the men who either don't understand or don't know how to handle the anger and frustration the restrictions arouse in women they deal with; and for the companies and managers who must find solutions for the problems at hand and build organizations to meet the new conditions.

EIGHT

THE CORPORATE RESPONSE

8

THE CHANGED PERSONAL and business relationships we see between men and women in today's offices are due largely to the women's movement and the sexual revolution. The changes have created new, challenging situations for corporate management. The old rules simply don't work under the new conditions, and while many companies are still trying, unsuccessfully, to apply them, others are beginning to address the issues raised by the growing presence and importance of women in the business world.

These attempts to translate today's sexual liberation into corporate terms are just beginning. Until much more is done in the workplace, the effect of progress made in the outside world area is diminished. Business may not be as important a part of American life as it was when Calvin Coolidge said "The business of America is business," but we still spend much of our waking time on the job, and what happens there, in terms of pay and prestige, affects the options open to us in our personal lives.

The most obvious sex-related problem today is harassment, so much company attention has been directed to eliminating it, or at least to complying with current legal requirements to do so. No company wants a big lawsuit for harassment or the resulting bad publicity. Some companies have tried to go beyond minimum compliance and look seriously at other, more subtle aspects of the changing work scene, such as the natural, noncoercive attraction that men and women employees feel for each other in work situations. As management consultant Jeanne Buffon Driscoll says: "I started addressing the issue of men and women working together not because of sexual harassment, but because of attraction. How do they manage their male/femaleness? Now, that's really a challenge. If it can't be met comfortably and productively, the possibility of men and women working together in productive fashion diminishes."

Driscoll, who heads the Driscoll Consulting Corporation in Williamstown, Massachusetts, with her husband Rick, made another point in an article she and Rosemary A. Bova wrote for *Management Review*. "As contacts with community organizations, churches, and extended families diminish, many people become socially isolated and find the work environment becoming the primary setting in which to meet people. All these conditions conspire to make it very difficult to follow the old maxim, 'Don't mix business with pleasure!'"

It is especially difficult, psychiatrist Robert Seidenberg noted, because "As people with interesting careers have always known, work is very sexy, and people with whom one is working are the people who excite. A day spent launching a project, writing a paper or running a seminar is more likely to stimulate—intellectually and sexually—than an evening spent sharing TV, discussing the lawn problems or going over the kids' report cards."

This kind of stimulation creates the sometimes disruptive feelings that Driscoll finds in her consulting work for companies such as General Electric, Olin Industries, and Polaroid. She usually deals with groups of workers from the same department, although people sometimes seek her advice individually. Feelings of attraction are rarely mentioned in group meetings, Driscoll told us, but they often come out in individual sessions. The employee, usually a woman, will confess that she feels strongly attracted to a co-worker, or her boss, and says that the feelings make it hard to do her job properly. Sometimes the attraction is mutual; sometimes it isn't. Either way, it is disruptive. What she wants to know is, What should she do about it?

Driscoll's advice is to evaluate the alternatives as cooly as possible. Look at the pros and cons of both the job and the man. If her feeling for the man is stronger, the best idea might be to look for another job and keep the man. If the job wins out, try transferring to another group or department in the company, if that is feasible. Otherwise, Driscoll believes, it is usually impossible to keep both the job and the man. The company is likely to transfer or fire one of you as soon as management becomes aware that the relationship is troublesome.

Driscoll told us that while executives at some companies have accepted the idea that attraction between co-workers is a legitimate area of concern, most are still skittish about getting involved. They'd like to improve male-female relations, or so they say, but what they really want is a quick fix: a film, a few meetings, and a list of recommendations that will help their men and women live together happily ever after. Unfortunately, fairy tales won't change attitudes or behavior that have been built up over generations. It takes a lot of work and a continuing commitment that most companies find difficult.

Even managers, personnel people, and affirmative action officers who are most sensitive to the need for strong action have trouble handling certain situations. A major area of uncertainty, they tell us, is the grey area between words and actions that one person thinks of as normal give-and-take between the sexes and another considers to be sexual harassment.

A woman who heads the personnel department for a large department store illustrated the difficulties by telling about two women who worked as secretaries for a marketing executive at the store. The man, in his mid-forties, was married to a successful account executive, whose job frequently took her out of town for days at a time. His first secretary, Sally, moved up after three years to become an assistant buyer in the sportswear department, a promotion her boss helped arrange. When the personnel director saw Sally in the elevator a few weeks after she changed jobs, Sally went out of her way to praise her old boss, and mentioned casually that she had gone to dinner with him the previous night, something she had done occasionally in the past when his wife was out of town.

With this as background, the personnel director was surprised when the man's new secretary, Marie, came to her three months later and asked if there was another job she could be transferred to. When asked why, she hemmed, hawed, and finally said she didn't want to become more involved with her boss; she wanted to work, not date. The personnel director asked if the boss had made any sexual advances to her or threatened to fire her if she didn't go out with him. In other words, did Marie feel he was harassing her? "Not really," she said. "But working with him has really become unpleasant the last few weeks. I guess I'd better tell you the whole story."

According to Marie, everything was fine for the first month until one afternoon her boss asked her out for a drink after work. Although the idea made her uneasy, she said she'd meet him downstairs. After an hour or so, she left. The next day, the boss walked by her desk just before five o'clock, said "I'll meet you in the bar," and walked out. Marie didn't want to go but felt she should. As she got up to leave after having a drink, he took her hand, saying, "Stay and have dinner with me. My wife is out of town and I'd appreciate your company." Marie said she was sorry, but she had a date with her boyfriend. They were meeting to talk about their wedding plans.

The man seemed stunned, Marie said, and then upset. "Great, you didn't tell me you were getting married when I hired you. I suppose that means you won't be around very much. I need a secretary who can spend some time with me, the way Sally did." Marie felt embarrassed and awkward. She didn't know what to say, and, after an uncomfortable silence, she walked out.

The following day, her boss was cooler than usual, Marie felt, but still cordial. This slightly strained atmosphere lasted a few weeks—until the man's wife left town again. He again suggested dinner, "to get to know her better," he said. When Marie refused, he stormed off. After that, things went from bad to worse. According to Marie, her boss acted coldly toward her and didn't talk at all except about business. Even then, he didn't give her any of the interesting work she had handled for him earlier.

Because the personnel director had been harassed on a previous job, she decided to press Marie for further details. Perhaps she was afraid to be frank about what had really happened. Had the man ever made sexual comments to her? Had he ever touched her in an intimate way? How had Marie felt about her boss during that first month, before he had asked her for a drink?

Marie insisted he had never made any suggestive remarks or gestures and that she had really liked him at the start. He was friendly and helpful, pointing out how what she was doing related to other departments and saying that the more she learned, the sooner she would be able to move on to a better job. "He was a great boss," she said, "until he wanted me to go out with him."

Before going any further, the personnel director decided to take Sally out to lunch and ask her directly about her relationship with the boss—the drinks, the dinners, and so on. Asked if she had ever had a date with her boss, Sally looked surprised, then said, "I guess so. We used to have dinner or drinks sometimes when his wife was out of town. I never thought of it as a date. He was just lonely. He loves his wife and we just had a good time together—like friends."

The other woman persisted. Had he ever made a pass at her? Sally became indignant. "No way. He was just friendly. What's this all about?" When she was told that Marie had asked for a transfer, and why, Sally shook her head. "She's crazy. He doesn't mean anything. He just wants a secretary who thinks of him first. And when his wife's away, he needs company. If Marie were smart, she'd keep working for him and accept the invitations. She'll learn a lot more about the business, and he'll learn a lot more about who she is and what she's interested in. There just isn't time enough during the working day to talk about the job or your future. I guess I was doing him a favor by keeping him company, but he sure repaid it by teaching me about the company and helping me get a better job."

To get all sides of the story, the personnel director then discussed Marie's feelings with her boss—again informally, over lunch. He was sorry she felt put upon, he said, but not surprised. Things just hadn't worked out. He needed a secretary he could feel close to and work closely with. Marie certainly should have her transfer if she wanted, with his blessing.

Marie got her transfer to a new job, the man hired a new secretary, and everyone seemed satisfied. But the personnel director still wonders if she did the right thing. The executive has had two secretaries since then, apparently without incident, but neither of them has been promoted, in part because his evaluation reports have been rather flat and noncommital. He hadn't gone out of his way to draw attention to them as he had for Sally and some of the other women in his department.

Whether he is angry about what happened and has decided to stop trying to gain recognition for the women who work for him, or whether the two secretaries he's had since then simply haven't had any special qualifications, the personnel director will probably never know. She still feels she might have been wrong in talking to him, or that she went about it in the wrong way. The problem, she told us, was that since there was no obvious harassment, she wasn't sure what to do. What she finally did might have cost other women a much-needed helping hand. But it might also have done some good by making the man realize that after-hours are not part of the working day and that no one should be punished, even indirectly, for wanting to keep their private lives private.

In another case, intervention by the personnel director was more clearly beneficial, although the harassment that caught her attention was unintentional. A young woman was hired as a lab assistant to a biologist in a research firm. The first morning, her new boss walked Lana around the lab and the business offices to introduce her to the people she would be working with. He kept his arm around her most of the time, and, according to Lana, introduced her with remarks such as, "Look at the goody I've got working for me," or "I really lucked out this time. I've got the prettiest assistant in the lab." At one office, a man asked if he could borrow Lana, "when she wasn't busy with her boss."

The remarks, Lana felt, were clearly sexist. As soon

as she got back to her desk, she went to the personnel office and broke into tears. She just couldn't work with men like that, she insisted, and asked if there was another job available. Since the company had just put out new guidelines on sexual harassment, the personnel director was called in immediately. She was quite surprised by the stir, since there had never been any complaints or even rumors about that department. She also knew the biologist personally and, so far as she knew, he was a happily married man—certainly not a womanizer or obvious chauvinist.

After calming Lana down, she told her there was an assistant's job open in another lab that was headed by a woman. She would try to get Lana a job there, if that's what she wanted, but the director wanted to speak to the biologist first. When she told him what had happened, he seemed genuinely shocked, then angry that his actions had been so misunderstood. As they talked, he gradually calmed down and left her office rather quickly after agreeing to the transfer, if it could be arranged.

Two days later, he came into the personnel director's office, closed the door, and told her, "You really opened my eyes the other day. I never realized that what I meant as friendly fun might be seen as insulting by someone who didn't know me or the others. And I guess I never would have made some of those patronizing remarks if my new assistant had been a man. As for putting my arm around Lana, I've always been a toucher—I guess that comes from having an affectionate family—but I'll watch it from now on. I certainly don't want to make anyone uncomfortable or unhappy."

In both these cases, the fact that the personnel people were women made them particularly conscious of the misunderstanding that can develop. They wanted to do more than just arrange a transfer and let it go at that. As one of them told us, "Part of my job is to help the people who work here understand more about each other so they can work better together. I try not to preach, but I feel I'd be neglecting my responsibilities to the company and to other women if I didn't do something to correct and improve things when I get the chance."

The same woman admitted that her strong stand against sexual harassment of any kind was made possible by the backing and positive attitude of the company's top management. "When you work for a company in which women are not respected and the top people pay only lip service to supporting the EEOC guidelines, you're bound to have a lot more harassment of all kinds, including that damned locker room humor. Under those conditions, women's complaints are simply not taken seriously, and anyone in personnel or anywhere else in the company who makes an issue of harassment or unequal treatment just won't last long."

According to other personnel people, the recent publicity about sexual harassment has had one unfortunate effect. Young women who are working for the first time, they tell us, often see any friendly gesture or kidding as harassment and overreact. This is embarrassing for everyone and usually has a negative effect on their future prospects by making their boss and the other people they work with feel uncomfortable.

"It's like crying for momma when a big nasty boy chases you home," says one personnel officer. "Some of these girls come in here every time a man looks at them. They better get a tougher hide and learn to get along with people."

This attitude—which in some cases is justified—still puts all the burden on the woman to adjust to "the way things are." It does not address the continuing, more prevalent problem of changing the way things are to guarantee that so many women will not, justifiably, feel threatened or humiliated.

Most of the other personnel and affirmative action people we talked to favor a less active approach to handling male-female relationships—other than overt harassment that they see themselves—until they are officially asked to investigate a complaint. What if an affair between two employees was causing dissension among co-workers, we asked? What would they do then? The answer was usually the same. If someone came and complained— for example, that a woman had been promoted unfairly or given better job assignments because of a romantic involvement with a boss or supervisor—the personnel officer would look into the situation. But from what most of them said, they seldom hear complaints of this kind. Employees prefer to go to an immediate superior or department head with the problem.

Personnel people are cautious about initiating action on their own, one personnel manager indicated, because relying on gossip or personal observation can be sticky: "I feel we're not here to monitor the sex lives of our employees. It's not our business what people do, so unless we are asked to become involved we stay out."

The methods companies have developed for promoting sexual harmony and dealing with sexual harassment are as diverse as the companies themselves. Some do little more than post the EEOC guidelines (listed at the end of Chapter 4) on an office wall. Others develop elaborate programs, with films and meetings for employees and special sessions for all levels of management. These sometimes include role-playing or other techniques to help managers recognize their own prejudices and failings as well as teach them how to handle complaints from employees.

Some companies have put in full-scale programs after being hit by employee suits. Others hope their programs will forestall suits by letting everyone know that top management is as opposed to sexual harassment as it is to racial or religious slurs and discrimination. Lawrence Vickery, general director of employment relations for the General Motors Corporation (GM), says: "In my opinion, there is no difference between sexual harassment and rape except that one is based on economic power and the other is based on physical power."

The program GM has developed for its managerial personnel is considered one of the most thorough in the country. As Vickery explains, "We knew that EEOC was looking at the issue of guidelines. They did turn them out in a kind of raw form, but a number of companies had already issued policy forms of their own and, quite frankly, we wanted to do the same thing.

"First of all, we put together a committee—mostly women, professionals, many of whom had at one time been secretaries. Then there were a few men, like myself, who had some responsibility in the area—affirmative action, that kind of thing. We brainstormed the possibilities over and over. We gave some information and ideas to our group at General Motors Institute, our engineering college, and they put together a training program."

Vickery says that the program was made mandatory for all supervisors, about 40,000 people. GM also developed a videotape which can be shown to small groups of supervisors and followed up with a group discussion of ideas and problems particularly pertinent to each group. To start things off, GM provides a list of typical questions and answers, such as "What's the difference between sexual harassment and acceptable kidding?"

"Our answer," Vickery says, "is that it should be determined by common sense. Dirty jokes, sexual slurs, comments upon the body are improper. Another question was, 'What about relationships people enter into freely?' The answer to that is, 'It is not our intent to interfere in cases like this. But if one of the people does not welcome the attention placed upon him or her, the potential for sexual harassment exists.' It is the supervisor's job to create an environment where people can come to him with these concerns and know they will be treated seriously and taken through the proper channels.''

Sometimes the problems are more a matter of habit and misunderstanding than anything else. Vickery offers an example. ''We have had women who hear a man call them honey—an older man from the South who has called women that all his life—and she thinks that is sexual harassment. We have to straighten that guy out and tell him that he'll have to find a different word even though he means nothing by it. It's his responsibility to be aware of how his behavior affects other people.''

Vickery stresses that any harassment program must be flexible. ''We don't give people a list and say you can't do this and you can't do that. We go more on the basis of determining how the person perceives a particular behavior. . . . We can't define what sexual harassment is in any hard and fast way because it's different for different people.

''All our managers in a particular office or working area must complete the training on a given day. Then a notice goes up announcing this fact, so all employees know they've completed the training. Now you've got a couple of interesting forces at work. You've got people who have been told this is how they are to behave; their job is to create an atmosphere that is free from sexual harassment. They are aware that the people they are responsible for have also been told about it. So everyone knows that sexual harassment is against GM's policy and we don't expect you to put up with it. If it happens, complain to your supervisor.''

Levi Strauss and Company, a firm that has had a reputation for harassment complaints in the past, has developed a training program to accentuate management's full support for its formal policy against such harassment. Gail Hale, who is director of planning and policy for the company, explains that they had put together several different versions of their training film after screening commercially produced films that are available on the subject. ''We developed some of our own vignettes,'' Hale says, ''which are typical for our company. For example, the training session we put on for the sales folks emphasizes situations that might occur in a sales environment.''

Hale emphasized a point we heard from executives in companies of all sizes. A strong corporate policy is vital, but it is only a start. ''The actual training is really important and needs to be done,'' Hale says. ''I've heard of situations in which a man came in laughing and sniggering out of the side of his mouth. After spending three hours in the training program, he came up to the trainer afterward and said, 'Wow, I never realized that's what I've been doing.' ''

Subtle hostility against women, particularly in fields that have long been male preserves, is another grey area that presents problems. Most management and personnel people say that such situations often aren't even brought directly to their attention because they are so hard to pin down. Rather than direct harassment, there is an insidious atmosphere of put-down, frequently expressed in the form of a seeming compliment or joke that puts a woman ''in her place'' without using words or actions that are obviously offensive.

A woman walks into a meeting and is asked to take

notes, or make coffee. Or perhaps someone comments on her appearance, with a leer implied if not expressed. Or the men are elaborately courteous or considerate: ''Now watch your language, guys.'' The kind of patronizing hostility is something that companies must counteract if they sincerely want to utilize the great potential women have to offer in the business world. It does no good to hire and promote women if they are not accepted by their co-workers, or if they are used as window dressing and denied a chance to prove themselves in open competition.

Some companies have tried holding consciousness-raising sessions for managers and supervisors, particularly in departments or areas of a company women are entering in large numbers. These can help—if both the top managers who set up the sessions and the lower-level people whose consciousness is the target really accept the fact that attitude changes are needed; and if the women involved understand that the men have problems, too, and need time to work them out. Many men are genuinely perplexed about how to treat women in new work situations and are doubtful about how far they should go in changing their old ways and encouraging fellow workers to change theirs.

No company wants to feel that their employees are children who must be taught how to treat one another. But to ignore the male-female changes going on in offices today, and the problems that go with them, is certain trouble. Since most men and women, unfortunately, don't know much about each other's feelings and beliefs, meetings that encourage a free exchange of views between them are an important part of any program. Mutual respect are the keywords—the basis for an understanding that men and women can work together, be friends, and even fall in love without causing personal or career problems for either of them.

Recent history shows that traditional misunderstandings can indeed be overcome. The improvement in black–white work relations over the past thirty years is striking proof of what can be done. We have a long way to go, obviously, but despite all the unfulfilled hopes, the progress is remarkable to anyone who remembers how things were. Many white workers have come to respect black workers—and vice versa—when the two have been encouraged (in many cases, forced) to work together on an equal basis. Men and women can certainly do as well. What is happening outside the office proves what can be done. While no one would maintain that we live in a non-sexist world, men and women today are relating more equitably outside the business world than they are inside it. It is time—indeed, past time—for corporations to emulate the liberation that is developing all around them.

Many choices come down, ultimately, to economics. Money and jobs are considerations that even the most biased can understand. From a corporate standpoint, it is bad business to allow sexual traditions or prejudice to determine the conditions people work under, or the opportunities open to them. And it is good business for companies that—based on corporate wisdom or government prodding—invest time and energy in training women to take the next step and create an environment that protects the investment and makes it profitable. Some companies are trying hard. Others are simply hedging their bets.

NINE

THE FUTURE: MEN, WOMEN, & WORK

9

SOME TIME SOON, companies will no longer see women in one way and men in another. On that day sex in the office will cease to be a potential problem and become instead a question of options and possibilities for each of us to answer personally.

But that is firmly in the future. Today, we are in the painful throes of transition. The old rules, rituals, and restrictions are being chipped away as women win grudging recognition of their rights and roles in the workplace. Old and new ways conflict and intermingle, creating situations that are confusing to everyone involved. Bringing order out of the chaos will take the cooperation of men and women on the job and at all levels of corporate management.

One major area of uncertainty in today's companies is the mentor relationship. Of all the man/woman interactions that take place in an office, this one has received a major share of the attention in recent years. Read virtually any "how to get ahead in business" book for women and, eventually, the magic word will appear. According to most of the books, a mentor—someone higher in the organization who shows you the ropes, sings your praises in the right ears, and gives your career discreet nudges in the right direction—is essential to success, especially for a woman. Without a mentor, it seems, you are merely another bright and hardworking employee— but still a loser. Delayne Gold, senior vice-president at Bache Halsey Stuart Shields, insists that mentors help only "if you perform well and create your own mentors. You can't just have someone pluck you up and pull you to the top."

In other words, a mentor can be useful if the relationship develops naturally. But for women, such natural development is hard to come by and even harder to maintain without creating problems for both people involved. Last year, the writers of a *Harvard Business Review* article interviewed 24 women managers between 26 and 48 years of age who said they had mentors at some time in their careers. The writers also spoke to 13 men, aged 36 to 66, who were then or had been mentors to women. Both groups worked for companies in the Northeast or Midwest in marketing, finance, and several other fields.

Most mentors agreed that the difference between sponsoring women and men was a matter of emphasis. At the beginning, when the protegé is at a low level in the organization, women need more encouragement than men, since they have less self-confidence in their ability to do the job; at higher levels, they need more "selling" by the mentor to convince others of their ability. As one mentor explains: "You can't underestimate the importance of having a chance to prove yourself. Women don't often get this, because they aren't given the benefit of the doubt. The risks in making a mistake are always higher for women."

What did the men get out of the relationship? Most talked about "putting back into life what you get out." Others stressed the organization's needs. "If you're going to create a top-flight organization, you have to have top-flight people. My chances of getting them are halved without women."

The article details some of the special problems created when the mentor is a man and the protegé a woman (or vice versa, although this is still rare). For the mentor, the authors say, sponsoring a woman is more of a risk because she is more visible within the managerial ranks. While a male protegé can fail quietly—"A young man can bomb without anyone noticing," according to one mentor—a woman's mistakes are often "broadcast." Two of the men we talked to said that, to protect themselves, they maintained higher standards for female protegés than for males.

The biggest problem for both mentor and protegé, of course, is suspicion by others that the relationship has more to do with sex than with business. This suspicion—accurate or otherwise—can damage both careers, as gossip about them and rumors of favoritism diminish job performances. And, as the *Harvard Business Review* article warns, home lives can also be affected, due to "the resistance of some wives and husbands to their spouse's close relationship with a member of the opposite sex—especially when the work involves travel."

Only three of the 24 women interviewed admitted having had an affair with the mentor, although several others felt that some sexual tension did exist. Most of the women believed it was mainly their responsibility "to behave professionally and learn to cope with any tensions or rumors that may arise (inevitably rise, according to some of them)."

A few of the men felt the responsibility was at least half theirs. As one said, "There is a greater tendency for sexual attachment when the mentor is supportive and the rest of the environment isn't. You'd be dumb not to think about sexual tension and rumors. It's always there. Professional conduct by both people is essential."

The danger of having a mentor relationship misinterpreted is one reason women are less likely than men to find mentors. Another is the fact that mentors frequently identify with the one they help, and it is obviously difficult for a 50-year-old man to see a younger self in someone wearing a skirt, however well tailored.

Another confusing area in today's changing office environment is the role of the token woman. She still exists—and still faces special problems. Being the new girl on a previously all-boy executive row or in a solidly male sales training program is never easy, on the new girl or the old boys. The woman is likely to find herself treated as a pushy intruder, a sex object, a servant, or all three, in various demeaning combinations.

The putdowns may be disguised as overwhelming courtesy or consideration. The new marketing director of a small plastics firm—we'll call her Eileen Smith—explains that when she first started presenting reports at company meetings, she would be greeted with remarks about "how cute it was to see such a tiny little thing spout all those big numbers." Other times the response would center on her dress or her hair style. "This would make me so mad," she says, "that I would start to turn red or feel tears in my eyes." These reactions only led to further remarks, such as how nice it was to have someone around who could still blush.

Eileen realizes that all this made her seem like something of a freak, and also affected how effectively she presented her report and how well it was received. She is still struggling with the problem, but she has developed a thicker skin. She seldom blushes any more and is determined to keep her job and win the respect due her ability.

Of course, many women would be willing to face these problems if they also got the job that goes with them, but that doesn't make the situation any less frustrating or unfair. Fortunately, some men are appalled by such discrimination and are willing to call other men on their words and actions. Sociologist Cynthia Fuchs Epstein, who has studied the problems faced by women lawyers, tells of an incident that illustrates how useful this kind of support can be to women who are being belittled in subtle or not so subtle ways:

"A woman lawyer reported sitting in meetings with her colleagues and clients who used salty language regularly. Every time they said something like *shit* or *goddamn,* they'd look at her and say, 'Excuse me, Lee.'

"This happened at several meetings. Then, one day after they had discussed the possibility of filing suit against a competitor, the client broke in angrily, 'All right, send the fucking subpoena. We . . . Oh, excuse me, Lee. I didn't . . .' One of the lawyers cut in quickly: 'It's O.K., Frank. Lee's heard of subpoenas before.' "

For some women, being a token female has its advantages. She is in the enviable position of working closely with a large number of eligible men, a situation that presents many opportunities for sexual dalliance, if that is what she wants or if she decides that playing the field is a way to gain acceptance and have some fun at the same time. Or perhaps she'll concentrate on one particular man, and end up with an office romance.

Francine Hall, professor of organizational behavior at the Whittemore School of Business and Economics and author of *The Two-Career Couple,* believes that such romances seldom work out well. "At the outset, you can be levelheaded in weighing whether career or lover comes first, but once you get involved, you forget all about this.

"The fact is that if two people in a company are very close, they are subjecting themselves to criticism. Even if it's two women or two men, if one of them is high up in the company, other people get jealous. One must recognize this political reality and conduct relationships so as to be above reproach and to avoid accusations of favoritism. You really have to walk that fine line so others won't have the opportunity to criticize.''

If you do have an affair, Hall suggests, remember that most companies still prefer a secret affair to marriage. ''If a couple are not married, and the company doesn't know about their relationship, there are no problems to deal with. Once two people in a company get married, there can be conflicts of interest and problems about confidentiality.''

Hall's recommendations are not unusual. Most of the books and articles advising women how to get ahead seem to come out against serious office relationships, usually for the reasons outlined by Hall. The problem with this advice is that it directs young women toward a one-dimensional life. To be successful, it seems, women must abandon the emotional side of their lives along with the friendship and camaraderie that men have generally considered an essential part of the good life.

We don't believe this call to office asceticism is necessary or justified in today's world. The advice is usually based on the experience of women executives who achieved success when it was much more difficult for women to get ahead. To ask young women to follow that same narrow pathway today does not fit the picture they have of their lives. They want both sexual freedom and career advancement, and expecting them to sacrifice one for the other is to deny their right to become complete individuals.

Devoting full time and energy to a job may even be self-defeating in purely career terms. Most companies want something more than one-sided drudges for their top positions. Thinking and planning to succeed in business alone shuts out part of the normal maturing process: the growing ability to love, to look beyond one's own needs to the needs of others. Such growth is as essential to being a good executive as it is to being a good friend or lover.

Clearly, men and women should be allowed to act like men and women in the office as freely as they do elsewhere, so long as they do their jobs and don't interfere with how others do theirs. If a relationship is equitable, it shouldn't be restricted or destroyed by obsolete company rules and attitudes or by the jealousy of co-workers.

This is not to advocate a sexual free-for-all. There are still too many chances for harassment and other exploitative use of sex in office relationships for companies to take a completely hands-off attitude. But rather than discouraging equitable relationships, whatever their sexual content, companies should encourage an atmosphere in which men and women respect each other's abilities and rights. If this takes some regulations and some company interference, so be it. Eliminating stereotypes and sex roles will go further in protecting workers' jobs and private lives than any rules about dating or marriage.

When American business and business people decide to treat sex in the office maturely, and respect the privacy of its practitioners, both the serious problems of sexual harassment and exploitation and the annoying fascination with the sexual lives of co-workers will cease to be problems in the office. We expect that, in tomorrow's offices, there will be more romance, more couples working together, and much less sexual harassment. Harassment is bred chiefly by inequality and misunderstanding—conditions that are far more costly economically and emotionally than sex and love will ever be.

INDEX

165

Index

Index